LAMENTATIONS

ABINGDON OLD TESTAMENT COMMENTARIES

LAMENTATIONS

DIANNE BERGANT, CSA

Abingdon Press
Nashville

ABINGDON OLD TESTAMENT COMMENTARIES
LAMENTATIONS

Copyright © 2003 by Abingdon Press

All rights reserved.

This book is printed on recycled, acid-free, elemental-chlorine–free paper.

Library of Congress Cataloging-in-Publication Data

Bergant, Dianne.
   Lamentations / Dianne Bergant.
     p. cm. — (Abingdon Old Testament commentaries)
   Includes bibliographical references and index.
   ISBN 068708461X (Bdg. : Paper : alk. paper)
   1. Bible. O.T. Lamentations—Commentaries. I. Title.   II. Series.
   BS1535.53.B465 2003
   224′.3077—dc21

                                  2002156116

03 04 05 06 07 08 09 10 11 12—10 9 8 7 6 5 4 3 2 1

MANUFACTURED IN THE UNITED STATES OF AMERICA

CONTENTS

Foreword 9

Introduction 13

Literary Characteristics 14

Acrostics 14

Voice 15

Genre 16

Poetic Features 17

Metaphor 19

Canonical Placement 20

Historical Considerations 21

Contents 22

Commentary 25

LAMENTATIONS 1: The Desolation of Zion 25

A Lament over the City: 1:1-11*b* 26

The Sorry Plight of the City: 1:1-6 27

The Cause of Such Unspeakable Distress: 1:7-11*b* . . 38

The City Itself Laments: 1:11c-22 44

Look, See, Hear: 1:11c-12 45

The Lord's Fierce Anger: 1:13-18a 47

Hear and Look: 1:18b-19 50

The City Prays: 1:20-22 51

LAMENTATIONS 2: The Destruction of the City 55

The Witness Cries Out: 2:1-19 55

The Wrath of God: 2:1-9a 56

The Anguish of the People: 2:9b-12 67

Zion Is Addressed: 2:13-19 72

Lord, Look What You Have Done: 2:20-22 77

LAMENTATIONS 3: The Strong Man's Lament 81

I Am the Man: 3:1-20 82

I Have Hope: 3:21-24 89

The Lord Is Good: 3:25-39 92

Let Us Return to the Lord: 3:40-47 98

I Am Lost—Hear Me: 3:48-57 101

Pay Them Back: 3:58-66 104

LAMENTATIONS 4: Society Has Collapsed 109

After the Fall: 4:1-16 110

Dashed Hopes: 4:17-20 120

Taunt Against a Neighbor: 4:21-22 122

LAMENTATIONS 5: The Final Petition 125

Remember, O Lord: 5:1-18 126

You Reign Forever: 5:19 131

Restore Us: 5:20-22 132

Conclusion. 137

Select Bibliography. 141

FOREWORD

The *Abingdon Old Testament Commentaries* are offered to the reader in hopes that they will aid in the study of Scripture and provoke a deeper understanding of the Bible in all its many facets. The texts of the Old Testament come out of a time, a language, and socio-historical and religious circumstances far different from the present. Yet Jewish and Christian communities have held to them as a sacred canon, significant for faith and life in each new time. Only as one engages these books in depth and with all the critical and intellectual faculties available to us, can the contemporary communities of faith and other interested readers continue to find them meaningful and instructive.

These volumes are designed and written to provide compact, critical commentaries on the books of the Old Testament for the use of theological students and pastors. It is hoped that they may be of service also to upper-level college or university students and to those responsible for teaching in congregational settings. In addition to providing basic information and insights into the Old Testament writings, these commentaries exemplify the task and procedures of careful interpretation.

The writers of the commentaries in this series come from a broad range of ecclesiastical affiliations, confessional stances, and educational backgrounds. They have experience as teachers and, in some instances, as pastors and preachers. In most cases, the authors are persons who have done significant research on the book that is their assignment. They take full account of the most important current scholarship and secondary literature, while not attempting to summarize that literature or to engage in technical academic debate. The fundamental concern of each volume is analysis and discussion of the literary, socio-historical, theological, and ethical dimensions of the biblical texts themselves.

The New Revised Standard Version of the Bible is the principal translation of reference for the series, though authors may draw upon other interpretations in their discussion. Each writer is attentive to the original Hebrew text in preparing the commentary. But the authors do not presuppose any knowledge of the biblical languages on the part of the reader. When some awareness of a grammatical, syntactical, or philological issue is necesary for an adequate understanding of a particular text, the issue is explained simply and concisely.

Each volume consists of four parts. An *introduction* looks at the book as a whole to identify *key issues* in the book, its *literary genre* and *structure,* the *occasion and situational context* of the book (including both social and historical contexts), and the *theological and ethical* significance of the book.

The *commentary* proper organizes the text by literary units and, insofar as is possible, divides the comment into three parts. The *literary analysis* serves to introduce the passage with particular attention to identification of the genre of speech or literature and the structure or outline of the literary unit under discussion. Here also, the author takes up significant stylistic features to help the reader understand the mode of communication and its impact on comprehension and reception of the text. The largest part of the comment is usually found in the *exegetical analysis,* which considers the leading concepts of the unit, the language of expression, and problematical words, phrases, and ideas in order to get at the aim or intent of the literary unit, as far as that can be uncovered. Attention is given here to particular historical and social situations of the writer(s) and reader(s) where that is discernible and relevant as well as to wider cultural (including religious) contexts. The analysis does not proceed phrase by phrase or verse by verse but deals with the various particulars in a way that keeps in view the overall structure and central focus of the passage and its relationship to the general line of thought or rhetorical argument of the book as a whole. The final section, *theological and ethical analysis* seeks to identify and clarify the theological and ethical matters with which the unit deals or to which it points. Though not aimed primarily at contemporary issues of faith and life, this section should provide readers a basis for reflection on them.

Each volume also contains a select bibliography of works cited in the commentary as well as major commentaries and other important works available in English.

The fundamental aim of this series will have been attained if readers are assisted, not only to understand more about the origins, character, and meaning of the Old Testament writings, but also to enter into their own informed and critical engagement with the texts themselves.

Patrick D. Miller
General Editor

INTRODUCTION

How lonely sits the city that once was full of people! (1:1)
Restore us to yourself , O LORD, that we may be restored;
   renew our days as of old—
unless you have utterly rejected us
   and are angry with us beyond measure. (5:21-22)

With these heart-wrenching words, the book of Lamentations opens and closes. The descriptions of grief and humiliation with which the poems are filled are graphic and the imagery employed is lurid. There is no attempt to hide the horror of the destruction that the people experienced. The reader is invited to ground-zero of the devastation, there to stand dumbfounded by the enormity of the collapse of this once glorious city and of the human tragedy that was left behind in its wake. While the account of grief is remarkable in its honesty, from a theological point of view, the apparent lack of resolution of the city's dilemma is troubling. Why has God allowed this to happen? Will God eventually relent and comfort the formerly highly favored city? Or are the city and its surviving inhabitants doomed to remain in the dire straits that the text so poignantly portrays? The book itself does not answer these questions. It is up to the interpreter to answer them.

There are two significantly different approaches to reading a piece of literature like the book of Lamentations. In one, a context is sketched into which the literary piece is placed and within which it is understood. Following this approach, one might summarize a likely historical scenario from the history of Israel, such as the time of the destruction of Jerusalem by the Babylonians (ca. 586/7 B.C.E.), and then interpret the poems that comprise the book in terms of that history. In the other approach, the literary piece is read first and clues for constructing its context are drawn from the piece itself. Following this approach, only data that are actually in the poems are used to chart a possible historical setting. The second interpretive approach is preferred in this study. In other words, nothing about Israel's history will be presumed if there is not clear evidence of it within the text itself.

LITERARY CHARACTERISTICS

Acrostics

The first and most obvious feature of this book is its literary structure. Although it may not be obvious in translation, four of the book's five chapters are arranged in the form of an acrostic, a pattern based on the twenty-two letter Hebrew alphabet. The first four chapters are true alphabetic acrostics, each verse beginning with a successive letter of the alphabet. In chapters 1, 2, and 4, only the first line of each verse begins with the respective letter; in chapter 3 all three lines of the verse begin with it. Although chapter 5 consists of a twenty-two-line poem, its verses do not follow the alphabetic pattern, and so it is not considered a true acrostic. However, its twenty-two-line length and its placement in the book of Lamentations continues the acrostic theme.

Although the alphabetic structure is clearly artificial and it restricts both the free flow of poetry and an ordered development of thought, adherence to it requires skill and ingenuity. Some commentators maintain that the acrostic is an aid to memory retention. All consider it a creative way of indicating comprehensiveness, its very structure suggesting that everything from A to Z is included. Its function within the book of Lamentations is twofold, implying (1) that the experience described elicited the total range of human grief and desolation, and; (2) that this emotional expression is controlled within the limits of the acrostic pattern. The fact that each chapter is a complete acrostic may be evidence of the literary independence of each poem in the book.

Voice

Several voices are heard in the poems. The first is that of the narrator, the individual who reports the disaster that befell the city. At times the narrator seems to relate the tragic events in a somewhat dispassionate manner (cf. Lam 1:1-11). At other times the narrator identifies with the suffering of the city and laments along with it (see 2:11). There is no way of knowing from the text whether this narrator is a man or a woman. Most commentators seem to imply that it is a man. This may be due to the fact that the narrator does not identify with the women when their plight is explicitly highlighted (see 4:10; 5:11). But then the narrator does not identify with any of the groups of men either (see 4:7, 13-16). Actually, it was usually the women who functioned as professional mourners (cf. Jer 9:17), and so there is no reason to presume automatically that the original figure behind this narrator was a man. However, since the society that produced the book was patriarchal (father-headed) in structure and androcentric (man-centered) in its perspective, most probably in the final form the narrator was male.

The second voice heard is that of Daughter Zion (see 1:6). The city itself, personified as a weeping mother, recounts her own destruction and cries out in grief. The female personification of cities is quite understandable. The first and most obvious reason is derived from the relationship between inhabitants and their city of origin. They are the ones who perceive the city as the mother from whom they come and upon whom they depend for survival. The history of cities is often told through the use of sexual metaphors. Cities are established and defended by men; their land is fertile and productive or barren and worthless; when their walls are penetrated, they are said to have been violated. Literature of the Ancient Near East shows that female personification of cities was both common and quite effective in such characterization.

A third identifiable voice is the man found in chapter 3. Since the Hebrew term can be translated "strong man," he will be referred to in that way throughout this study. Traditionally, this man has been identified as the prophet Jeremiah. This may be because the personal anguish that the man describes in this chapter corresponds to the suffering of that well-known prophet (cf. Jer 9:1; 15:10-18; 20:7-18). However, more recent scholarship is of the opinion that this man is a representative figure of the typical sufferer. In some verses he speaks as an individual "I" (see 3:1-39); in other places he seems to speak as the collective "we" (see 3:40-47).

Finally, there is the poet. Which voice within the text represents the voice and perspective of the author? Some commentators think that the narrator is really the veiled voice of the poet. However, there is no solid evidence on which to base this position. In fact, it is possible that the poet is really recounting the devastating experience of destruction from several points of view—from the perspectives of the female mourner (narrator), the personified city, and the strong man. This would explain both the apparent inconsistencies within the book as well as the repetitions. The one voice that is never heard, the voice that would explain the purpose of the devastation and the accompanying desolation, the voice that would bring comfort, is the voice of God. Throughout the misery and anguish, the accusation and entreaty, God is silent.

Genre

Three different literary types or genres have been uncovered in the book of Lamentations: the dirge, the lament, and the city-lament. While there is disagreement among scholars as to the primary genre of the various poems, many interpreters acknowledge the mixed-genre character of the book in general and of various of its poems as well. Characteristics of the dirge include: an opening cry of desolation; a summons to mourn; a declaration that death has occurred accompanied by the eulogizing of the deceased; a description of reversal of fortune; an expression of the mourner's grief; a reference to the effect that this death is having on the passersby; an expression of bewilderment at what has happened. The standard lament possesses the following elements: an invocation of God's name; a description of present need; a prayer for help and deliverance; reasons why God should hear the petitioner; a vow to offer praise or sacrifice when the petition has been heard; an expression of grateful praise.

Yet a third classification, known as the city-lament, has recently been gaining acceptance among scholars. One of its most striking characteristics is its personification of the devastated and agonizing city. Tribulations endured by various groups of inhabitants are portrayed. The collapse of civil order and the cessation of religious celebration are described from the perspective of those who have been conquered rather than that of the conqueror. Finally, it clearly states that the suffering has been divinely directed. More than forty years ago, Samuel Kramer, a well-known Assyriologist, noted similarities between the depiction of the goddess Ningal who weeps over the destruction of her sanctuary and that of personified Zion who, in the book of Lamentations, sits weeping among the ruins of the city. He even went so far as to suggest that city-laments were the forerunners of the book of Lamentations. Since that time there has been disagreement concerning the degree and character of influence that these Mesopotamian works exerted over the Hebrew book. Comparative study of the Mesopotamian literature and sections from both the Hebrew prophets and the psalms reveals elements of this genre that pre-date Lamentations. Hence scholars conclude that a native city-lament genre probably existed in Israel, to which the book of Lamentations has been assigned. It seems that Israel did not need the Mesopotamian works as models for its own city-laments.

Poetic Features

In the Western world, we are accustomed to think of poetry as speech organized in measured lines. This is not the case in all cultures. For example, Hebrew poetry contains characteristics that make it quite distinctive. It is particularly noted for its terseness. Several features contribute to this: it uses few connecting words such as conjunctions; it is rich in parallelism, a kind of correspondence of one thing with another (see 1:5*a*); it employs ellipsis, the tendency to drop a major theme from the second part of a poetic line, expecting the reader to carry the sense of that theme over from the first line (see 5:11); its imagery embodies multiple meanings in concise forms.

One specific poetic characteristic of the book of Lamentations is the metrical pattern of each line. While there is not perfect metric uniformity in the poems, one pattern seems dominant. In it, the line falls into two distinct parts, the first part being longer than the second. With one beat accorded to each word or phrase, the line contains a 3 + 2 pattern. Since this pattern generally appears in laments, it has come to be called the *qinah* or lament meter. (Though other metrical patterns occasionally appear, 3 + 2 remains the basic meter.) The irregularity of the beat suggests a kind of choke or a sob, a gasping for breath as one would do in extreme situations. This meter has been characterized as a kind of limping rhythm, one that seems to die away. Although all of the verses of the poems do not fit easily into the *qinah* pattern, the high percentage of those that do argues against rejecting the *qinah* characterization outrightly, as some commentators have done.

Parallelism is a prominent feature of Hebrew poetry. The essence of parallelism is correspondence of one reality or aspect of reality with another. This correspondence takes the form of either equivalence or opposition. The equivalence or contrast can be grammatical, based on parts of speech, or lexical—based on word pairs. The semantic dimension of parallelism is the relationship between the meaning of one line and that of its parallel line. Either one thought can substitute for the other, or the second line builds on the first and together the two lines contain a semantic progression of thought.

As with all poetry, biblical verse employs various poetic devices. Chief among them are simile and metaphor ("How like a widow she has become" [1:1*b*]). Hyperbole, the deliberate use of exaggeration for the sake of effect ("For vast as the sea is your ruin" [2:13]), and personification, the assignment of human characteristics to inanimate objects ("She weeps bitterly" [1:2*a*]), heighten the imaginative quality of verse. Hebrew poetry is noted for its play on sounds: alliteration, the repetition of beginning sounds whether of a consonant or a vowel; consonance, the repetition of internal consonant sounds; and assonance, the repetition of internal vowel sounds ("panic and pitfall have come upon us, devastation and destruction" [3:47]). Other poetic devices include: *inclusio,* the repetition of words or a phrase at the beginning and the end of a poetic unit ("therefore, I have hope" [3:21-24]); and merism, polar word-pairs that include everything between the poles ("Whether they sit or rise" [3:63]).

Metaphor

Probably the most significant poetic feature of the book of Lamentations is its use of metaphor. Most metaphors compare two different objects in order to uncover the presence of a particular characteristic which is obvious in one of them, but not in the other. Every metaphor consists of three elements: the vehicle, the member of the comparison to which the characteristic naturally belongs; the referent, the member about which the comparison is made; and the tenor, the analogue or actual characteristic of comparison. For example: "He is a bear lying in wait for me" (3:10). Here, the predatory nature (the tenor of the metaphor) of the bear (the vehicle) is attributed to God (the referent).

The relationship between the vehicle and the referent is usually representational. This means that a feature of one object represents a feature in an otherwise unrelated object. However, there is another way in which metaphors function, a way that produces meaning by juxtaposition rather than comparison. In this second or presentational way, the association of ideas is based on emotional response rather than physical similarity. Viewed from a presentational perspective, the metaphor from the book of Lamentations used above generates terror. In that passage, the poet is intent on describing the destruction of the city (representational) as well as producing an emotional reaction to its devastation (presentational).

CANONICAL PLACEMENT

The placement of the book of Lamentations within the entire biblical corpus influences the way it is understood. In the Hebrew Bible, known as the MasoreticText (MT), the books are arranged under three headings: the Law, the Prophets, and the Writings. There the book of Lamentations is found among the Writings. However, it occupies a different place in Jewish liturgical practice, where it belongs to a collection known as the Megilloth or Minor Scrolls. This collection consists of five books that are used during the liturgy on various feast days. The Song of Songs is used on the eighth day of Passover, Ruth during the Feast of Weeks or Pentecost, Ecclesiastes during the Feast of Tabernacles, and Esther during Purim. Lamentations is read on the 9th day of Ab, the fifth month of the Jewish calendar. This day, which commemorates the two destructions of the Temple in Jerusalem, falls in late summer between the feasts of Pentecost and Tabernacles. The Megilloth order of the books follows the Jewish liturgical calendar, thus placing Lamentations between Ruth and Ecclesiastes. As a liturgical text, the book continues to play an important role in the Jewish community even to our day.

In the Septuagint (LXX) or Greek translation of the Bible, the books are arranged quite differently. There Lamentations follows either the writings of Jeremiah or those of his secretary Baruch, whenever this latter book is considered canonical. Many Christian denominations incorporate readings from the book of Lamentations in their Holy Week services. It should be clear that when this is done, the message of the book is thereby given a Christian meaning. In the Greek version, the placement of the book with the writings of Jeremiah or with those of Baruch (see Jer 36:4) reinforces the dating of Lamentations at or about the time of the Babylonian destruction of the city of Jerusalem in 587 B.C.E.

The singular nature of chapter 3 is obvious to all who read the book. Although it is as long as are chapters 1 and 2, its acrostic structure is more complex. In addition to this, it contains the poignant cries of an individual sufferer rather than the description of the city's anguish. Furthermore, it is only in this chapter that one can detect a ray of hope. Various theories have been advanced to explain this distinctiveness. Though controversial, the view adopted here is based on the *qinah* structure. The similarity in structure of the first three chapters resembles the first three beats of the lament meter, while the abbreviated chapters 4 and 5 resemble the *qinah*'s shortened beats. This approach to understanding the book retains the character of the lament and reinforces the sorrowful note on which the book ends.

HISTORICAL CONSIDERATIONS

Until the recent past, interpreters thought that the poems in the book of Lamentations were composed in Palestine in response to the political, social, and religious crisis precipitated by the defeat of the Israelites and the destruction of their central city Jerusalem (587 B.C.E.). Many connections have been made between the scenes painted in the chapters of this book and the description of that city's tribulations as found in other biblical material. For example: the breach of the walls of the city of Jerusalem is described elsewhere (4:19; 2 Kgs 25:4-5) and the infidelity of the prophets is deplored (2:14; Jer 5:31). One cannot deny the influence that this disastrous defeat made on those who endured the catastrophe and survived to tell of it. In various places, the poems themselves identify the city as Zion/Jerusalem. Although there is mention of Edom, one of Israel's oldest enemies (4:21-22; cf. Obad), the fact that rivalry between these two nations covers a vast segment of their history prevents us from using this reference as a signpost for dating the book. The same might be said about the reference to Egypt and Assyria (5:6). Egypt was probably Israel's oldest foe and a pact to elicit its assistance could have been made at almost any time after Israel's settlement in the land. Unless Assyria is used in a metaphoric sense, mention of it argues against an exilic dating, because at the time of Israel's exile that nation no longer existed.

While Israel's defeat and exile was clearly a deciding factor in the development of its tradition and in shaping the contours of its theological imagination, the metaphorical imagery found in these poems suggests that there might be more here than simply the description of one tragic episode. What happened at one time in history has been carefully shaped in such a way so that it can act as a figure or type for describing the tribulations endured during other tragic events, such as the destruction of Dresden or Hiroshima or Dubrovnik.

Identification of the author of the book is closely linked with the decision about the date of its composition. Until recently, tradition held that the poems came from the prophet Jeremiah. This contention is based on a statement about Jeremiah's lamentation (cf. 2 Chr 25:35). Even if the book did originate at the time of the Babylonian exile, there is no sure evidence that Jeremiah was its author. If, on the other hand, it is a later literary composition, then authorship cannot be attributed to the prophet. Most scholars today subscribe to the anonymity of the author. While in many ways there is great similarity among the poems, this does not rule out the possibility of multiple authorship. The unique structure, content, and perspective of the communal lament in chapter 5 itself sets this poem apart from the others and suggests a different author. Whether or not the poems came from the same hand, the repetition of vocabulary and the interweaving of various themes suggest that the final editing certainly did.

CONTENTS

Each of the five chapters has its own distinctive character. Chapter 1 consists of a city-lament proclaimed by the narrator (1:1-11) followed by the city itself lamenting her fate (1:12-22). In chapter 2 the narrator speaks again, describing the destruction of the city and the anguish endured by her inhabitants (2:1-19).

This second poem ends with words from the city directed toward God (2:20-22). A new voice is heard in chapter 3. A strong man describes the torments that he himself and a communal "we" have endured (3:1-66). Many maintain that this communal "we" and the narrator are really the voice of the community. The narrator speaks again in chapter 4 (4:1-16), this time identifying himself with the suffering inhabitants of the city (4:17-20) and hurling a taunt at a faithless neighboring nation (4:21-22). In the final and shortest chapter, the narrator once again speaks generally about the city's afflictions (5:1-22).

COMMENTARY

LAMENTATIONS 1

THE DESOLATION OF ZION

The intricacies of the structure of this first poem reveal the extraordinary artistic acumen of the poet. The most obvious and overarching feature of the poem is its acrostic organization, each verse beginning with a successive letter of the alphabet. Also, the 3+2 *qinah* meter predominates throughout. Yet another feature of the poem is the length of its verses, three lines to a strophe, with the exception of 1:7, which contains four lines.

The very complexity of this first poem lends itself to various methods of division and analysis. While insights gleaned from various approaches will be incorporated in this investigation, the principle of division employed in this commentary will be that of voice. Two voices are heard in this poem. There is the narrator

(1-11*b*), the voice that describes the scenes of destruction and misery, not to be confused with the poet who is responsible for the entire composition, and the city, personified as a woman, the victim of the misfortunes (11*c*-22). Each of these speeches is interrupted once: the city breaks into the speech of the narrator (v. 9*c*) and the narrator interrupts the city (v. 17). The following is the structure adopted here:

1-11*b*	narrator
9*c*	(city)
11*c*-22	city
17	(narrator)

A Lament over the City: 1:1-11*b*

Literary Analysis

It is very difficult to determine the exact genre of this poetic unit. It possesses certain features of the dirge, such as the introductory exclamation "How" *('êkāh),* third person speaker, and descriptions of the reversal of fortunes. However, unlike the funeral elegy, it is not a response to death, for though many, if not most, of her inhabitants have been put to death, the city herself survives to mourn her loss. Nor is there an invitation to join in a mourning ritual. Rather, it is a description of a city that, though despoiled and depopulated, weeps over her tragic situation. In this, it resembles a plaintive lament, and it possesses various features of that genre: (1) an expression of grief resulting from a national disaster; (2) a description of how the suffering affects the way the city views herself and her status in the broader society; (3) her relationship with God; and (4) a direct plea to God to take notice of the city's affliction.

Despite all of these genre similarities, this passage fits best into the classification of the city-lament. The most obvious characteristic that it shares with this genre is its personification of the destroyed and agonizing city. Other features include the description of the tribulations endured by various groups of inhabitants, the collapse of civil order and the cessation of religious celebration described from the perspective of the conquered rather than the conqueror, and finally, the clear statement that the suffering has been divinely directed.

Each strophe in this unit consists of three lines, with the exception of verse 7, which has four lines. Scholars divide the unit in different ways, following various criteria. Although there is thematic overlapping, which will be noted throughout the commentary, the material seems to fall into two major sections:

1-6   description of the sorry plight of the city
7-11*b*   explanation of the cause of such unspeakable distress
9*c*   prayer to God by Jerusalem

THE SORRY PLIGHT OF THE CITY

Exegetical Analysis

The narrator begins this speech in the same way as both the second and the fourth speeches begin, with a mournful cry traditionally associated with the dirge: "Ah!" or "Ah how!" ('*êkāh*; see Isa 1:21). This single word bespeaks astonishment, incredulity, horror. It introduces a description of reversal of fortunes, one of the foremost characteristics of the both the funeral dirge and the city-lament and perhaps the underlying theme of this poem. This startling word is followed in rapid succession by three sets of contrasting descriptive phrases: once filled with people, the city is now lonely; once great among the nations, she is now a widow; once a princess among the provinces, she is now a vassal. The first two lines (v. 1*ab*) contrast the city's present deplorable state with her former greatness. The order of the third line (v. 1*c*) is just the opposite; reference to her former royal nature precedes the declaration of her present servitude. With this shift, the strophe begins and ends on a note of desolation.

By means of personification, a trait of the city-lament, the city is characterized as a mother, a widow, and a princess. Maternal personification of cities was a common ancient practice that has survived in many places even down to the present day. Probably the major reason for such characterization stemmed from the fact that ancient cities were generally walled. The image of residents within its confines corresponds to that of children within the womb of their mother or, upon their birth, within the circle of her maternal care. An examination of the myths of origin of many cities of the ancient world reveals the belief that the inhabitants of the city were born from the union of a patron god and his consort, who may be either human or divine. Identification with the mother may have been easier than with the father, because there may not have been certainty about paternity while people generally knew the mother from whom they had been born. In societies where survival of the people was a major concern, female fertility was considered one of its most valued possessions. These considerations may explain why large cities were regarded as fertile mothers.

The metaphor of mother implicit here functions in the following way. Mother is the vehicle of the metaphor, the carrier of the meaning that is to be transferred. The city is the referent of the metaphor, the receiver of the meaning. The tenor of the metaphor or the point of comparison, is maternal fertility. In this first poem, the city mourns over her reversal of fortune. The female characteristic of maternal fertility, so highly valued in the ancient world, was originally enjoyed by her. She was "once full of people." Now, however, the opposite is true. She is alone. The metaphor tells us that the city is childless, that is, devoid of inhabitants.

Widow has a slightly different meaning than the previous characterization. In patriarchal societies, women are under the legal jurisdiction and protection first of their fathers and then of their brothers. When they marry, their husbands assume this responsibility. Upon the death of their husbands, their sons do. When the Bible speaks of widows, it generally refers to those who have no legal protector and, therefore, are vulnerable and defenseless. They have no male relative to act on their behalf. In this instance, the intended tenor of the metaphor is probably the vulnerable status of the woman rather than the absence through death of her husband. In former days the city may have enjoyed being "great among the nations" (v. 1*b*) because of her numerous children, but now she is alone and unprotected like a childless widow.

The final contrast contains two metaphors: princess and vassal. The meaning of the first metaphor is obvious. Just as a princess is of royal descent and enjoys the power and privilege that accompany such lineage, so the city once occupied a position of dominance among neighboring cities and it commanded their respect. Now the reverse is true. She has become the vassal of another. This metaphor suggests that now she is captive, a prisoner of war, one who owes homage and fealty to an overlord, one subjected to forced labor.

Metaphors function in two ways, a representational manner which highlights physical similarity and a presentational manner intended to elicit an emotional response. While both functions are operative here, the presentational manner seems to be dominant. This is confirmed by the introductory mournful exclamation "How" *('êkāh)* and the vivid depiction of reversal of fortune, as well as by the use of hyperbole in the descriptions themselves: "full of people . . . great among the nations." The narrator is not content merely to report the plight of the city. This report is meant to startle the onlooker and cause dismay.

The personification of the city continues (v. 2). She is desolate and grieving. Although the last line of this strophe contains a distinct dirgelike statement of reversal, the general description more closely resembles that of the city-lament. It is a description of misery, not of death as would be the case in a true dirge. Overwhelmed by sorrow, the city weeps and sheds tears. Though frequently used interchangeably, these two emotional responses (sorrow and weeping) are not exactly the same. The word for weeping denotes convulsive gasping for air and crying aloud for relief. It is frequently accompanied by tears, as is the case here. Mention of night suggests desolation, and it implies that the city has been robbed of sleep and the strengthening refreshment that it affords. In the midst of the reversal of fortune and the devastation that it has brought, the city finds no comfort. This theme appears throughout the poem like a refrain (see vv. 9*b*, 16*b*, 17*a*,

21*a*), accentuating the hopelessness that attends the actual catastrophe. The city must endure unimaginable tribulation, "with no one to comfort her" (v. 2*b*).

The suffering city is not simply alone, she is desolate because her lovers have deserted her. Lover is a very provocative metaphor. It suggests an opening of oneself to another and the acceptance of the other in return. It can also imply passionate commitment. There has been significant discussion about the identity of these lovers. Some argue that this is a figurative reference to questionable political liaisons, dallying with foreign nations, or idolatrous cultic allegiance to other gods. Others maintain that it is merely a reference to those to whom the city was somehow appropriately committed. This statement of reversal might be even more tragic than the ones reported earlier: here her intimate friends are now her enemies. The poetic balance between "all her lovers" and "all her friends," with the latter's statement of reversal, helps us to realize that the actual identity of the lovers is not the issue. Rather, though not strictly expressed, an implicit statement of reversal appears in the second line of this verse as well. The beleaguered city may have enjoyed the attention and support of lovers in the past, but, whoever they might have been, they now offer her no comfort. The city is not only the subject of vanquishment and despoliation, but she is also the victim of abandonment and betrayal by those whom she should have been able to trust and turn to in times of danger and need.

It is not until the third strophe (v. 3) that the identity of the city becomes clear; for it is there that Judah is mentioned. If Judah is the nation, then surely Jerusalem is the city that was once great but is now desolate. Judah, which like the city is a collectivity, is here also the subject of personification. However, this personification is slightly different. It seems that the city sits where she always sat, but now she sits alone, while the nation Judah has gone into exile. It is important to remember that poetry by its nature is impressionistic and not meant to be analyzed in the same way as is prose. Overlapping of images and apparent inconsistency of thought are often present. An example of this inconsistency can be seen in the characterization of the city as a childless widow. If the inhabitants are dead, one is hard-pressed to say that the city is really still alive. Yet this city is alive, mourning the death of her children.

Judah was the name of the southern kingdom during the period of national division (922–722 B.C.E.), which the northern kingdom alone retained the name Israel. With the fall of the north, the south regained governing prominence and the name Judah incorporated the entire nation. It is in this inclusive sense that the name is meant here. Furthermore, while the name certainly identifies the political entity, the description here suggests that the reference is to the nation of people. However, the statement of reversal with which the strophe opens allows for both meanings. Judah the political entity has lost its former independence and is now in exile in the land of and under the jurisdiction of another nation; Judah the nation of formerly free individuals has been uprooted from its home and now lives in servitude to another.

The Hebrew construction of the first line of this strophe (v. 3a) yields two very different versions. If the preposition is translated as causal, it means "because of suffering and hard servitude"; if it implies a condition, it means "with suffering and hard servitude." The distinction is quite significant. The first version seems to say that the hardship was itself the reason for the exile. This suggests that Judah chose to be a fugitive in order to escape adversity. The second and more favored version indicates that the nation experienced hardship even before being taken into exile. This meaning is more in keeping with the sense of Judah's vulnerability before her oppressors and with the description that follows.

One of the divine promises made to the ancestors of the people of God was possession of a land of their own. The people cherished this land as a resting place, a place where they could be free from the tyranny of other nations (see Deut 12:9; Ps 95:11). Now, having been wrenched from her own land, Judah lives in exile among other nations with no resting place of her own. The third line of this strophe (v. 3c) appears to be out of chronological order. Surely the city's adversity ("her pursuers have all over-taken her") preceded her deportation (v. 3*ab*). However, poetry follows different rules than does prose narrative, and adherence to the poem's acrostic structure takes precedence in this ordering. Judah's pursuers were probably those who besieged her before she was taken into exile. This confirms the idea expressed in the first line of the strophe. The meaning of the Hebrew of this last line (v. 3*c*) is uncertain. The word frequently translated "dis-tressed" comes from the word for "narrow" or "cramped." It suggests that her pursuers overtook Judah because she was caught in a place which provided no opportunity for escape. Since each strophe adds a dimension to the description of the plight of the city, one can say that she was vanquished and despoiled, abandoned and betrayed; the nation was ripped from the security of her resting place and taken into exile.

The city once again demands our attention (v. 4). Strictly speaking Zion is the name of the mount upon which the city of Jerusalem was built. However, eventually the name of the city and that of the mount came to be used interchangeably. It is clear that this poem is talking about the city. The first line and part of the second treat features of the city itself; the rest of the strophe begins a consideration of the suffering of various groups of the city's inhabitants. Since the temple, the center of Israelite wor-ship, was situated in Jerusalem, the city itself certainly partici-pated in the celebrations of all the major religious festivals. Religious pilgrims would have crowded the streets; visitors would have filled the inns; and shops would have realized an abundance of business. The entire city would have been charged with the excitement of the feast. But Zion has suffered a reversal. Its roads are deserted, for the city has been ravaged and festiv-ities have come to an end. The roads themselves now mourn this loss of festive excitement.

The narrator next speaks of the gates of the city (v. 4*b*), an indication that it was indeed walled. City gates were very impor-tant for several reasons. First, they offered protection from inva-sion or stealth. Second, it was through them that the city was able to carry on commerce and the exchange of the fruits of civilization. Third, because of all of this activity, influential men conducted the major business of governance in the open square in front of these gates, giving the gates themselves added importance. Now they are said to be desolate. This word can mean "deserted," making the phrase a simple description of the empty square. It can also mean "disconsolate," adding to the emotional impact of the metaphor of personified gates. Both the roads and the gates grieve over the absence of religious pilgrims and the excitement that they brought to the city.

As is characteristic of a city-lament, the narrator calls attention to two groups within the populace, namely, the priests and the young maidens (v. 4bc). The cessation of ritual celebrations would have been particularly bitter for the priests, for the religious practices to which they had committed themselves and which were the source of their very livelihood have come to an abrupt end (cf. Joel 1:9). It is understandable that they would groan. There is evidence that young girls also played a significant role in ritual festivities, participating through song and dance (see Ps 68:25; Jer 31:13). The Hebrew here is uncertain. The same verb yields the meanings "grieve" or "thrust away." While some commentators argue that the line states that maidens are dragged away into exile, the context argues for the first meaning; just as the priests groan, so the young girls grieve. The narrator succeeds in recounting the overall bitterness experienced by the city.

The recital of reversal of fortune continues. The city's enemies have become her masters (v. 5). This suggests not only defeat but also humiliation. It calls to mind the promise of dominion over others as a reward for fidelity to the commandments of God, and the warning of subjugation to them as a punishment for faithlessness (see Deut 28:13, 44). The issue of reward and punishment was a constitutive element in Israel's understanding of covenant, always regarded as a unique, sacred, and binding agreement between God and the people. Within the context of covenant, God promised divine protection and expected obedience in return. This notion of covenant was fundamental to Israel's self-understanding. The commandments, with their attendant rewards and punishments, were less restrictions on the behavior of the people than guides meant to show them the way to live within this covenant relationship.

The statement of reversal is followed immediately by an explanation of the real source of the city's misery, as well as the reason for it (v. 5b). As is the case with the city-laments, the deity is responsible for the suffering of the client; the LORD, the God of Israel, has caused her this unspeakable grief. (The personal name of the God of Israel appears here for the first time.) Why has God acted in this way? Because of the city's many sins. The word for sin used here originates in the political realm and means "rebellion," not simply mistake nor violation of social or ritual prescription. It designates the casting off of prior allegiance to a ruler. From a religious point of view, it implies that the city has rebelled against her God. Despite the extent of the city's tribulations, it would not be correct to say that God has been excessive in punishing her. The plural form of the word for sin indicates that she has rebelled many times. In a certain sense, the seriousness of the covenant commitment requires that God act in this way. Up to this point, the poem has described only the plight of the city; there is no clear indication of guilt. Here, the explicit statement of guilt clearly declares her culpability. Her transgressions were serious, and so her punishment is severe.

The LORD has used a foreign nation as an instrument of divine retribution. Not only do her foes become her masters, but they prosper at her expense. Once again the poem intimates that the city remains. It is its inhabitants, her children, who are taken into captivity. Poetic overlapping appears in the statement about Judah the nation of people going into exile (v. 3), and that of the inhabitants or children of the city of Zion going into captivity. What a heart wrenching scene this paints! The word for children comes from the Hebrew word for suckle, suggesting the intimate bond that exists between the city and her inhabitants. In the past she nourished them from the substance of her own being. They were suckling infants, totally dependent upon her. Snatched from her embrace and her protection and forced into exile, they are now captives of the enemy. This loss of children is not only a present tragedy, but it also signifies the forfeiture of the city's future. This is a heavy price to pay, but the city's repeated rebellion calls for such harsh measures.

Though not an actual statement of reversal, the city's loss of splendor or majesty is both a serious blow and a humiliating circumstance (v. 6). Here and elsewhere the narrator refers to the city as Daughter Zion, a epithet also found in the writings of Jeremiah (6:2, 23). One is tempted to ask: Daughter of whom? Throughout the book of Lamentations, Zion is characterized as a grieving mother. How then can she also be Daughter Zion? In answer to this question, we might note that the weeping goddess in the Mesopotamian city-lament genre is also frequently referred to as the daughter of some god. It may be that the Hebrew poet(s) incorporated this second characterization when the metrical pattern that was being followed in the verse was incomplete and another beat was necessary. The word *daughter (bat)* provides another beat and serves such a metrical purpose.

A report of the suffering of a third group of inhabitants (v. 6*bc*) is added to that of the priests and the young girls, continuing this feature of the city-lament. The Hebrew word that identifies this group yields the translations "princes" or "leaders." If the first translation is chosen, it would refer only to the members of the royal house, but their high station would emphasize the indignity of their disgrace (see Jer 39:4-5). The second translation would include a larger number of leaders and would underscore the broad scope of the humiliation suffered. These leaders, whether royal or otherwise, are compared to stags that are weakened by the lack of pasturage and thus unable to escape their pursuers. They are now hunted down like desperate animals. The reversal here is as disconcerting as have been all of the others. Those who were the leaders are now the pursued. Furthermore, theirs is a hopeless attempt at escape, for they do not have the strength to accomplish it. They are not only enfeebled, but they are also humiliated. The city and her inhabitants were unprepared for the sufferings that they were forced to endure. Each aspect of this devastation seemed outside of the realm of possibility and cut to the core of the city's sense of herself. How could this possibly have happened?

Theological and Ethical Analysis

This first section (1:1-6) raises three very important theological issues: the question of suffering itself; the theme of retribution; and the ethical issues surrounding the destruction of a city. From the very introductory exclamation of grief through the entire description of the city's devastation, the theme of suffering claims center stage. This passage does not address the origin or purpose of suffering, only the fact of it and its repercussions in the lives of those who suffer and those who witness it. Suffering is a human experience known by all, and all are forced to come to grips with it many times during the span of life.

Too often suffering can take hold of human consciousness and completely reshape the self-understanding of sufferers. Even if they are normally confident and productive, when they suffer intensely, they can become lost and despondent. Layer after layer, the supports of life seem to collapse, and they feel as if they are left to sit alone and in utter misery. The cries that break forth from Job (see Job 7:1-16; 10:1-3; 16:1-17) and from the psalmist (Pss 55:1-11; 102:1-11) attest to this. Suffering can literally drain the life out of them, and the repeated assaults that they may be made to endure at its hands can leave them in a state of hopelessness. There may be no escape; there may be no easing of the pain; there may be only suffering. This poem bears striking resemblance to the siege and destruction of the city of Jerusalem at the hands of the Babylonians (see 2 Kgs 25:1-7). Still, the descriptions found here can also serve as metaphors which characterize other kinds of suffering, suffering with which many people can identify.

The first response of many in the face of such tragedy is to cry out for help. However, as was the experience of the city, the sufferers' relationships with others are often the cause of or they contribute to their misery. Their claim of being oppressed by others may not be an empty claim; they actually may be the victims of attack and betrayal. For them there may be no outstretched hand to help; no understanding voice to console; they frequently are at the mercy of those who show no mercy. On the other hand, the reverse could be true; they themselves may perpetrate such suffering in the lives of others. It is no wonder that life has been referred to as a "vale of tears." Intense suffering frequently calls for a reexamination of priorities, values, and aspirations. Suffering always raises theological and ethical questions such as: Why do bad things happen to good people? Can any good come out of suffering?

Besides turning to others in the midst of affliction, many people turn to God. Often misfortune throws light on their understanding of God and of their relationship with God. His relationship might be that of a loving parent who is tenderly concerned for human welfare: "Can a woman forget her nursing child?" (Isa 49:15), or it might be a stern judge responsible for the balance of order on the world: "[The LORD] stands to judge the peoples" (Isa 3:13). This passage from Lamentations clearly delineates the city's relationship with God. The reason given for her suffering is infidelity to her covenant responsibilities. The covenant was a legal concept. Those who entered into covenant were bound together in a unique form of intimacy, enjoying certain rights and entrusted with certain responsibilities (see Exod 19:4-9). The idea that God was Israel's covenant partner is the basis of its understanding of God.

By her own admission, the city has been seriously and consistently unfaithful to her covenant commitment. This point raises the theme of retribution, which holds that reward will come to those who are good, while punishment will be the lot of the wicked (see Deut 7:12-15). Although this theory does indeed often provide a genuine explanation of the some of the tragedies of life, it still generates some serious questions. It may serve as an incentive for righteous living and as a deterrence for wickedness, but it is not a satisfactory criterion for interpreting all of life's painful situations. Even if the inhabitants of the city did sin grievously, the element of proportionality questions whether the degree of infidelity of which they were guilty warranted total destruction, the punishment of those who had been loyal along with the reprobates. This reservation brings to the fore the issue of theodicy, the human effort to vindicate a good God in the face of what appears to be injustice. This issue plays a very important role in the drama that unfolds in the book of Job: If God is just, why does such tribulation befall the righteous? This passage from Lamentations may not address the question of theodicy, but the reader cannot avoid asking it.

This image of the anguished city is certainly a picture from the distant past. However, to view it only in that way would be very shortsighted, for within the recent past the fate described here has shattered too many other cities. Throughout the world and down through the ages, cities have suffered betrayal, invasion, plundering, despoliation, and grief with no consolation. The picture of Daughter Zion appears in today's newspapers and on television screens all too frequently. This raises the ethical question of one's responsibility toward those who have been struck down by calamity. Care for the needy is a work of charity, as is solidarity with the victims. Israel's Deuteronomic covenant law requires that such care be shown to those in need (see Deut 15:7-11). This responsibility flies in the face of the treachery of enemies, the betrayal of friends, and the indifference of dispassionate bystanders described here in Lamentations.

THE CAUSE OF SUCH UNSPEAKABLE DISTRESS: 1:7-11b

Although the lament over the condition of the community continues in these verses, there is a decided shift in focus. The first verses paint a picture of the city's distress. This section describes the appalling circumstances that brought about that deplorable situation.

Exegetical Analysis

In their attempt to make all of the verses of the next strophe (v. 7) conform to the three-line strophe pattern, many scholars argue that the third line in this four-line strophe is a gloss, and they prefer to drop it. Other experts regularize the length of the strophe by balancing longer lines with shorter ones. Thus, though the pattern diverges, they retain the overall length of the strophe without unnecessary emendation. However, most translations retain four lines.

The actual name of the city finally stands out clearly: it is Jerusalem. The first verse of this section (v. 7) sharply contrasts the independent and prosperous life she lived in the past with the deplorable situation in which she finds herself in the present. The affliction that she endures is not merely suffering; it is suffering brought on by another. Jerusalem is the victim of assault. The Hebrew here is unclear. The word is rare and its ambiguity has led some scholars to substitute another more common word by changing one letter. The letters in question are ר and ד. The letters in question are similar in appearance, and so it is possible that there is an error in the manuscript and a correction should be made. The first reading yields "wander," and is in keeping with the idea of the inhabitants being taken into exile. In this option Jerusalem would be remembering her wandering. The poem, however, shows that the city herself did not endure the sufferings of exile, but rather, her inhabitants did. The second option yields "sorrow" or "bitterness," a word that certainly conforms to the general sense of the line and does not raise the question of displacement of the people. As tempting as it may be to correct the text in favor of precision, a rule in textual criticism insists that the more difficult word is probably the original one. Furthermore, poetic expression often includes apparent inconsistency. Therefore, "wandering" is the preferred translation here.

It is in such piteous straits that Jerusalem laments the glorious and satisfying days of old, remembering all of the precious things that she formerly cherished and enjoyed. There is no mention nor even a hint of what these treasures might have been. They probably included the marvels produced and enjoyed by a prosperous city, such as Jerusalem once was. They might also have included political and religious buildings and their furnishings, as well as stable social structures and institutions. Finally, every group of people holds dear hopes and dreams for the future. Jerusalem would be no exception here, but would cherish such hopes and dreams.

COMMENTARY

The downfall of the city is complete. The people are conquered, falling into enemy hands, and there is no one to help her.
Those who loved her have abandoned her and her friends have
betrayed her (v. 2). In addition to her defeat, the city must
endure the ridicule of her enemies. It is not clear whether the
enemies who deride her are the ones who defeated her or are
enemies in general. What really matters is the ridicule that she
must endure. In a society where matters of honor and shame
play such a major role in both self-identity and social status,
derision itself is often more deplorable than the actual reasons
for the derision. The city has collapsed and now her enemies
gloat over her. It is possible that at the heart of the city's lament
over her defeat is a more pointed lament over her humiliation.

The theme of the city's sinfulness, introduced earlier (cf. v. 5),
takes center stage in the present examination (vv. 8-9b). The word
for *sin* (v. 8) is a general term and means "miss the mark." The
Hebrew expression indicates the seriousness of the sin. Jerusalem
has failed to fulfill her covenant responsibilities and she is now
suffering the consequences of her own betrayal. The word translated "mockery" *(nîdâ)* is found nowhere else in the Bible and so
there is some question about its exact meaning. However, most
scholars believe that it comes from the word for "wandering to
and fro," suggesting a shaking of one's head in derision. This
interpretation corresponds to the mocking that was previously
mentioned (v. 7). The word itself sounds very much like another
Hebrew word *(niddâ)* which denotes ritual uncleanness caused by
menstrual blood, a theme that appears in the next strophe. Thus
this one word links three strophes. The connection that this creates suggests that the city's uncleanness, whether ritual or
metaphorical, is the reason for the derision that she must endure.

The honor and shame theme reappears in the form of a reversal:
those who honored the city in the past now despise her. The sight
of her nakedness is the reason given for this turn of events.
Nakedness, specifically the baring of genitalia, is not only associated with sexual arousal. It was also a form of humiliating punishment (see Hos 2:3). It was meted out to women guilty of sexual
impropriety (see Ezek 16:39) and, in order to shame them, con-

querors often took vanquished people into captivity stripped of their clothing (see Isa 20:3-4). In a passage that is surprisingly similar to this poem, the prophet Isaiah mocks virgin daughter Babylon, predicting that her nakedness will be uncovered and her shame will be seen (see Isa 47:1-3). This degradation is more than Jerusalem can bear. She can only groan and turn away in disgrace.

Once again the narrator asserts the sinfulness of Jerusalem, here characterized as menstrual blood clinging to her skirts (v. 9). These stains are signs that the blood that held the promise of life has been sloughed off as useless. Not only is the city unclean because she is in the ritual state of *niddāh*, but the stains on her clothing make her impurity plain for all to see. It appears that in the past she sinned with abandon, giving no thought to future consequences. For this reason, her fall from honor was dramatic and astonishing. Once again the poem states that there is no one to comfort her. A kind of *inclusio*, a set of boundaries that encircles a literary unit, sets off the description of the circumstances within which the city finds herself:

v. 7c   there is no one to help her

v. 9b   there is no one to comfort her

In the face of these frightful circumstances, Jerusalem interrupts the words of the narrator and cries out to God, the only one who might offer her help or comfort: "Look at my affliction" (v. 9c). By implication she is really saying: See and do something about my affliction.

The voice of the narrator returns to describe further the plundering of Jerusalem's treasures and to report the desecration of her temple (v. 10). Earlier in the poem, Jerusalem remembered all of the things that were precious to her (v. 7). Here the narrator states that the city's enemies have seized these precious things. An even greater blow to the city was to watch the holy places in the temple be overrun by foreigners. There are other biblical passages that describe the Babylonian invaders carrying off the most treasured cultic objects of the Israelites (see 2 Kgs 25:13-15; Jer 52:17-23). Thus, within the context of this description, the precious things might well have included or even specifically consisted of the treasures of the sanctuary.

The major part of the temple in Jerusalem was comprised of series of courts. Progressively, from the outer to the innermost court, entrance became more restricted until only the high priest entered the holy of holies, and that privilege was exercised only once a year on the Day of Atonement (see Lev. 16:2). Non-Jews could not proceed beyond the outer Court of the Gentiles (see Ezek 44:9). Israel maintained that the very structure of the temple was a divinely ordained replica of the cosmos, and violation of the restrictions that governed access to it was a threat to the very stability of the universe. Jerusalem's invaders thrust aside any regard for such majesty. Foreigners who never joined the company of the congregation (see Deut 23:3) defiled the sacred precincts of the sanctuary, and Jerusalem was forced to watch.

The consequences of Jerusalem's sin were very costly for her. She has suffered mockery (v. 8), the shame of defilement (v. 9), the desecration of the sanctuary (v. 10), and now famine (v. 11). The circle of those who groan enlarges. First it was the priests (v. 4), then the city (v. 8), now all of the inhabitants. They are in desperate straits, foraging for food, like animals. Their desperation is so acute that in order to revive their lives they are willing to trade what is most precious to them for food. Earlier verses stated that the city's enemies either destroyed or carried off her treasures (vv. 7, 10) and so the reference here must be to something else. It is probably either to the personal possessions of the city's inhabitants or, as a later report of cannibalism suggests, the reference here is to their children. It is on this desperate note that the words of the narrator conclude.

The scope of this pitiful situation is seen in the repeated use of the inclusive word "all." All of her lovers have abandoned her, all of her friends have been treacherous (v. 2), and all who once honored her now despise her (v. 8); all of her pursuers have overtaken her (v. 3), and all of her gates are desolate (v. 4); she has lost all of her majesty (v. 6), and all of her precious things (vv. 7, 10). The poem states that Judah has gone into exile (v. 3), Zion's children are now captives (v. 5). Yet, there are people left who forage for food. Such apparent inconsistency is probably poetic depiction intended to emphasize the depths of suffering endured rather than to provide accurate description of the events which occasioned that suffering. The city is desolate and her heart torn from her. There may be hyperbole in the language used in this city-lament, but there is no exaggeration in the intensity of the experience described.

Theological and Ethical Analysis

This section (1:7-11*b*) addresses in more detail the question of retribution. In this poem there is no doubt about the culpability of the city, hence the themes of innocent suffering and theodicy, or the vindication of divine justice in the face of injustice, need not be treated here. However, the relationship between behavior and the circumstances in life calls for consideration. This relationship forms the basis of the theory of retribution as well as that of justice. Sometimes this relationship closely follows a pattern of cause-consequence and there is no need to question why certain situations have arisen as they have. For example: "Hatred stirs up strife" (Prov 10:12); "One who forgives an affront fosters friendship" (Prov 17:9). In instances such as these, action is closely followed by an understandable consequence. The experience of life demonstrates the truth of such proverbs.

At other times it is difficult, if not impossible, to trace consequences back to their causes. At such times, people can feel subjected to the whims of chance, and they might begin to question either the wisdom of a God who created such an erratic universe (see Job 24:1), or the goodness of a God who allows human beings to flounder within it (see Ps 10:1), or the power of a God who has no control over the ebb and flow of life (see Jer 5:19). Furthermore, the one who suffers frequently must endure an added burden, namely, a sense of shame. In those situations where there is little or no question about culpability, this shame may spring from an interior realization of guilt. However, whether guilty or not, the suffering itself causes a sense of public shame. The one suffering can feel like "a laughingstock" (Job 12:4).

The biblical tradition insists that God created an ordered universe (Gen 1:1-25), that God is indeed good (cf. Pss 25:8; 34:8), and that God does exercise control over every aspect of the created world (Job 38–39). With this as the basic worldview, it is easy to understand why people look to human behavior as the reason for suffering, and why they see this suffering as either the direct result of human folly or as the sentence that God passes on human sin. The first explanation (the result of foolish behavior) may at times be close to the truth; people do in fact often bring on their own suffering. On the other hand, the second explanation (divine retribution) paints a picture of God that is harsh and vindictive, a picture that corresponds to the image of a wrathful God (see Exod 22:24).

There is no easy way of understanding human suffering. The very fact that the biblical tradition contains so many and such contradictory explanations of it is evidence of the complexity of the question. What is important is that people deal with suffering in a way that does not result in hatred or despair, but one which might strengthen and refine the human spirit (see Wisdom 3:6). It is easy to subscribe to such a valiant way of living, but it is difficult to learn how to live in such a way. Many of the major religions of the world grapple with this dilemma. In doing so, they exhort their members to endure suffering with courage and grace so that they might be purified as gold is purified in fire, that they might be strengthened as athletes are strengthened during workout, that they might be fashioned into works of art as silver is fashioned in the hammering. Such exhortation does not answer the theological question "why?" but it does address the moral question "how?"

THE CITY ITSELF LAMENTS: 1:11c-22

Literary Analysis

The second half of this chapter exhibits many, though not all, of the features of the plaintive individual lament. It opens with a petition addressed to God (v. 11c), which is followed by an invitation to the bystanders to "look" and "see" the sufferings that the city must endure (v. 12*a*). The major part of the lament consists of a listing of the city's tribulations (vv. 12*b*-18*a*). The narrator interrupts once (v. 17). Next, the city invites bystanders to hear and to see her sufferings (v. 18*b*). The unit ends with a double-wish prayer (vv. 20-22). These characteristics appear in the following structure:

> 11*c* petition to God
>> 12 invitation to look and see her sorrow *(mak'ôb)*
>>> 13-18*a* list of divine actions that caused the city's suffering
>> 18*b* invitation to hear and see her suffering *(mak'ôb)*
> 20-22 the double petition to God

Concentric structuring frames the core of this poetic passage: petition forms the outer frame (vv. 11*c* and 20-22); an invitation to consider the city's plight forms an inner frame (vv. 12 and 18*b*); the core of the passage is the description of the sufferings that God has heaped upon Jerusalem (vv. 13-18*a*).

The concluding prayer itself contains several characteristics of the lament. These include an invocation to God and a plea to take heed (v. 20*a*), an accusation against God (v. 21*b*), an acknowledgment of guilt (vv. 20*b*, 21*b*), complaint against enemies (v. 21*ab*), and a plea to execute reprisals against them (v. 22*ab*). The desire for such reprisals is a characteristic that the individual lament shares with the city-lament.

LOOK, SEE, HEAR: 1:11c-12

Exegetical Analysis

Twice the suffering city cries out the plaintive plea: "Look!" The first entreaty is directed to God: Look and see! (v. 11*c*); the second calls to all those who pass by on the road: See and look! (v. 12*a*). Each plea requests something of the one or ones to whom it is directed.

The lament opens with an appeal to God: Look! Take heed! See how worthless I have become! This declaration of dejection implies that the city was not always in such a sorry state. She has *become* worthless. There is no clue regarding the criteria she uses to judge her value, or lack thereof. However, the previous strophes list all of the ways she has been stripped, making her worthless by most standards. She has lost her independence, her populace, her status among the other nations, the sanctity of her sanctuary, her friends and lovers, and everything that she held precious. She has nothing of value, and so she sees herself as worthless. It is in this state that she cries to God: Look at me! Don't you turn from me too! See what has happened to me! Take pity on me! It is not that God is unaware of what has happened to the city. On the contrary, the LORD is the very one responsible for her tribulations (v. 5). The city wants God to see just what these tribulations have done to her, the depths to which she has descended. She cries to God, hoping for compassion.

The city directs the same plea to those who pass by on the road, though in Hebrew it is in the reverse order (v. 12a). Addressing people in this way is a very common feature in laments (see Ps 89:41). Normally, however, these passersby hurl insults and mockery at the one suffering. This does not seem to be the case here, for the city invites them to behold her desolation. She would hardly invite more scorn. The meaning of the two Hebrew words with which the address begins is unclear. The short phrase "Not to you" yields various translations. First, as a simple declaration, it responds to possible mockery from the passersby: This does not concern you. Second, as a rhetorical question it challenges their apparent disinterest: Does it not affect you? Third, as a wish it expresses a hope for them: May this never happen to you. What follows this phrase is a heart-rending petition: "Look and see if there is any sorrow like my sorrow." The city believes that her misery is beyond compare and she turns to others, hoping for caring eyes and empathetic hearts.

Jerusalem knows the source of her sorrow. Enemies may have overrun her and despoiled her, but it was really the LORD who inflicted all of this upon her. She draws from the prophetic tradition, characterizing her suffering as the Day of the LORD, a day of judgment and doom. Several of Israel's prophets spoke of this fearsome Day. The first reference to it appears in the writings of

Amos (5:18-20). He warned his audience that this Day would be one of judgment for them. The tone of his message suggests that they were anticipating a time when their enemies would suffer defeat and they themselves would prosper. Amos declared that, because of their sinfulness, that Day would be a time of judgment for them as well. Other prophets took up this theme (see Isa 2:12; Jer 46:10; Joel 1:15). Zephaniah described at great length the terrors of the Day (chapter 1). However, it was Ezekiel who spoke specifically about the destruction of Jerusalem on "the day of the wrath (burning fury) of the LORD" (7:19). Now the city interprets her ordeal as the unfolding of the horrors of that dreaded Day.

The Hebrew word for "anger" is the same as for "nostril." The image evoked by the expression "fierce (burning) anger" (v. 12c) is quite graphic. Blazing eyes are frequently a manifestation of anger, but so are flared nostrils. It is common knowledge that enraged animals frequently snort before they charge. The metaphor that the city employs here elicits the image of an angered God with flared nostrils, snorting fury. The Day of the LORD may have symbolized for Israel the most severe, even relentless, judgment of God, but it did not believe that this day would mark the end of all things. Israel believed that this judgment was the necessary purification that preceded the inauguration of a new age, an age of restored friendship with God. Although here Jerusalem's use of the theme concentrates on the destructive nature of the Day, the other, optimistic dimension of the Day remains in the background as a possible seed of hope.

Jerusalem perceives this Day in a way very different from that found in the prophets. They spoke about it as a time in the future. They warned their people of its advent in order to induce them to reform their lives and thereby avoid its threat. For the city, this Day is in the past. It has already come with all of the fury that it could muster. It has certainly destroyed the city, but has its burning anger purified it? And is there any hope for a better future?

The Lord's Fierce Anger: 1:13-18a

Exegetical Analysis

In rapid succession, Jerusalem cites various ways in which the Lord has afflicted her. All of the verb forms indicate that it was God who sent fire, set a trap, impeded her, left her desolate, yoked her, handed her over, made light of her strong men, celebrated her defeat, smashed her young men, and crushed her (vv. 13-15). There is no particular order to this listing of divine assaults, one of which would have been enough to convey the horror of the experience. Taken together the entire array reflects the magnitude of the ordeal. In order further to convey a picture of destruction and dismay, Jerusalem uses metaphors frequently found in both laments and descriptions of the Day of the Lord.

The first metaphor, fire (v. 13*a*), suggests both a literal and a figurative interpretation. During the assault on the city, the invaders most likely set fire to it. This fire came from on high, very much like the fire and brimstone that destroyed the sinful cities of Sodom and Gomorrah (see Gen 19:24; Ps 11:6). Though the fire was set by her enemies, it was really God who sent it. The tenor or meaning of the metaphor is both the destructive and the punishing nature of the fire. It penetrated the very bones of the city, its inner structure. Following this vivid image is a second one, a net (v. 13*b*). Since it was used to snare birds, animals, and fish, it lent itself as a metaphor for capture (see Ezek 12:13). It suggests subterfuge on the part of the one who sets the snare and helplessness on the part of the one snared. The quarry is not only caught by the net, but in being caught it has been out-smarted and, therefore, it is shamed.

During the siege that brought her down, Jerusalem was unable to advance in any way, because the Lord impeded her steps, turning her back at every opportunity. The Hebrew word translated "faint" in the last line of the strophe (v. 13*c*), refers in other passages to menstrual infirmity (cf. Lev 12:2; 20:18) and, therefore, implies ritual impurity. With this connotation to the word, the line might better indicate that the city was desolate rather than merely stunned.

Jerusalem continues her accusation against God with another metaphor, the yoke (v. 14). A yoke, made of either wood or some kind of metal, was placed on the neck of a dray animal. As a metaphor, it generally implies servitude (see Jer 27:8). That is its connotation here. God fashioned Jerusalem's yoke out of her own sins, and it was the magnitude of those sins that weighed her down. Having fettered her in this way, God handed her over to her conquerors.

Jerusalem recounts what happened to her mighty men and her young men (v. 15). The first group probably represents warriors, those responsible for her safety; the second is the hope of her future. The Lord has cut down both groups. The warriors of Israel were generally considered the warriors of God, fighting for the cause of God. Such is not the case here. Instead, God has stood against the city's mighty men, thwarting their efforts. Three images that characterize God's actions originate in the realms of agriculture and viticulture respectively. Harvest was a time of bounty, and the people celebrated this bounty with religious festivals. The imagery here is striking. God appointed a festival *against* the city, not *for* it. God cuts down the city's young men like sheaves at harvesttime and then threshed them to pieces. God trods down the nation itself as though it were ripe grapes in a winepress (Isa 63:3-4), the juice resembling the blood that ran in the streets. Judah is characterized as a "virgin daughter" (v. 15c). This metaphor suggests various tenors or meanings. Used for a nation as it is here, it could mean that as yet no other nation has entered Judah. In this sense, the invasion of her enemies would violate her. The intended tenor or meaning of the metaphor could be the nation's reproductive potential rather than her sexual innocence. In that case, the metaphor would imply that God has crushed the promise of future fecundity. Actually, the metaphor is so rich that both tenors are probably operative here.

The city weeps bitterly, having been forced to witness all of the tragedy described above (v. 16; cf. v. 2). Once again she complains that throughout her ordeal there has been no one to comfort her (vv. 2, 9); there is no one to bring back her spirit, her life force. The text states that her children (the Hebrew has "sons") are desolate. Earlier it was the city herself that was desolate (v. 13). And why is this the case? Because her enemies have prevailed against her.

The narrator interrupts the city's lament (v. 17), and sketches a picture of a desolate Zion stretching out her hands in a gesture of supplication. It recalls an earlier scene where the city pleaded for sympathy: "Look and see if there is any sorrow like my sorrow" (v. 12). However, as has been the case each time she sought solace, "there is no one to comfort her." The name "Jacob" appears. This was the name of the younger son of the patriarch Isaac. Jacob was the ancestor whose name was changed to Israel (see Gen 32:28). When the nation was known as Israel, the names Jacob and Israel were used interchangeably. During the period when the nation was divided (722–922 B.C.E.) Israel became the name of the northern kingdom. After the defeat of the north, it became the name of the entire surviving nation, though the accompanying name "Jacob" is often found in poetic writings such as this.

In yet another reversal (v. 17b), the poet describes how those around Jacob have become his enemies (v. 2). This is probably an allusion to neighboring nations such as Ammon, Moab, and Edom. Israel's relationship with them was always tenuous. They have now turned away from Jerusalem because of her uncleanness. The reference (niddâ) is once again to ritual impurity caused by menstrual blood. The city is defiled and her fair-weather neighbors do not wish to defile themselves through contact with her.

Jerusalem completes her recital of hardships with an admission of guilt (v. 18a). Although she insists that it is really God who has afflicted her, she does not blame God for the afflictions. She declares that the LORD is in the right. She is the one who has been wrong. Earlier the narrator accused her of sin (vv. 5b, 8a). Jerusalem herself has already admitted her culpability (v. 14a). Here she repeats that admission; through her sinfulness, she has brought on her own afflictions.

HEAR AND LOOK: 1:18*b*-19

Exegetical Analysis

The city cries out a third time: "hear and look"! (v. 18*b*). This cry is addressed to anyone who will hear. Jerusalem does not try to hide her devastation and resulting shame. Instead she exclaims: Listen to me! See my suffering! As described above, this half line acts as the second part of a frame. It is in the verses within the frame (vv. 13-18*a*) that the city cries these words so that all can hear and paints this picture of herself so that all can see.

What follows in the last line of this strophe (v. 18*c*) and in the next strophe (v. 19) conforms to the framing technique, repeating many of the themes found in earlier verses. The city laments the captivity (5*c*) of her maidens (4*c*) and her young men (15*b*). She had called out to those who loved her (2*b*), but they were unfaithful. Her priests (v. 4*b*) and her elders (her leaders? v. 6*b*) have perished as they searched for food (v. 11*a*). Here for the first time Jerusalem speaks explicitly of death. This last complaint provides a new insight into the city's horrific plight. Her ordeal was protracted, for death by famine is not swift. Furthermore, in such straits, it is the infirm who are usually the first to succumb. The fact that this is the fate of the city's religious and political leaders, citizens who usually enjoy relative prosperity, reinforces the idea of an extended period of desperation. Stripped of everything, the city cries out for pity.

THE CITY PRAYS: 1:20-22

Exegetical Analysis

The prayer that brings the first poem to conclusion opens with the familiar imperative: See! (v. 20). As was the case earlier (v. 11*c*), the city turns to God for compassion. Her distress has invaded her body and penetrated the very depths of her being. The ancients believed that the seat of emotion was situated in the bowels, while the heart was generally thought to be the seat of understanding.

Together, as they are here, they symbolize the totality of the city's inner turmoil. She immediately takes full responsibility for her distress. She has rebelled; she has disobeyed; she has brought it all upon herself. As a result, she is encompassed by God's fierce justice. The sword of conquest has cut down her inhabitants in the streets. Those who have survived this bloody horror are not exempt from death, for it has come unbidden into their homes as well (see Deut 32:25; Jer 14:18; Ezek 7:15). Death pervades the entire city.

Once again Jerusalem cries out against those who have heard of her misery and have done nothing (v. 21). They offer no comfort (cf. vv. 2, 9, 16, 17). In fact, they delight in her tribulation (vv. 7, 8). This time she does not rest with mere complaint. Rather, she calls down the wrath of God on their heads (vv. 21c-22b). Referring again to the fearsome Day of the LORD, the terrors which she herself has had to endure, she hurls an imprecation at them: "Let them be as I am;" Let them suffer as I am suffering! Let them experience reversal of fortune as I have! This is not simply a cry for vengeance. It is also a call for divine judgment: Let the Day of God's justice fall upon them as it has fallen on me! Jerusalem perceives this dreadful Day as an event in her city's past, but also one in the future of her enemies. Clearly Jerusalem believes that the justice of God is comprehensive in scope and no one can escape it. In this poem there is no remembrance of past favors that might ignite a spark of hope; there is no suggestion that things will change. The poem ends on a note of pathos: "My groans are many, I am sick at heart" (v. 22c).

Theological and Ethical Analysis

Three theological issues stand out in this second unit (1:11c-22): complaining to and about God; looking to others for comfort; and calling down the wrath of God on enemies. The view that God is all-good, all-knowing, and all-powerful, valuable theological tenets in their own right though not really biblical, have led some to believe that religious people should never complain about the way life unfolds. According to this point of view, to do so would be to question God's goodness, God's wisdom, or God's power.

Lamentations challenges this view. It demonstrates that it is not only quite natural to complain, but complaining to God springs from a dimension of faith. First, complaint to God is an admission of human vulnerability and need, and it is a turn to God in such a situation. In addition to this, it often flows from the conviction that God is indeed concerned about what is happening in the life of the one complaining, and that God has the power and the will to change the course of events. This is certainly an attitude of faith found in various places within the biblical tradition, particularly in the laments (see Pss 5:1; 17:1-2; 22:4-5; 43:1; 86:1-2).

While complaining *to* God might be understood as a form of trust in divine solicitude in the face of human limitation, complaining *about* God is probably more difficult to appreciate. However, in the Bible it too originates from an attitude of faith, one that is rooted in the covenant tradition and in the certainty that God exercises control over all things. Convinced of God's power, the one suffering might, like the Psalmist, complain about God's apparent disinterest (see Ps 10:1). Further in that prayer of complaint (vv. 12, 17-18), the psalmist appeals to God in confidence, convinced that God is indeed interested in human life with all of its projects and undertakings. Were this not the case, the one afflicted would probably not bother turning to God.

In this poem from Lamentations, Jerusalem complains bitterly both to and against God, but nowhere is she censored for doing so. This suggests that such complaint is not an issue for the poet. However, one cannot help wondering whether or not Jerusalem will continue to turn to God for compassion if God does not soon intervene on her behalf. The question of "How long?" is not a idle question. It is raised again and again in the Psalms (Pss 6:3; 13:1-2; 35:17; 79:5; 89:46; 90:13). How long will this city be able to endure? If there is no relief, will she turn away from God, perhaps even turn against God? The poem does not answer these theological questions—but it does suggest them.

Again and again Jerusalem looks to others for comfort, and she finds none. She does not ask for exoneration, only for comfort. This raises the question of the moral responsibility of offering solace to others, especially when it is sought. As is so often the case with ethical matters, this issue is not clear-cut. Under the circumstances described in the poem, it is fair to wonder how far sympathy and reassurance should be extended. After all, the city has admitted her guilt; through the violation of her covenant commitment, she brought on the hardships herself. Justice demands that she should pay the consequences of her failings. However, it is fair to wonder whether or not she should be left on her own. Having been stripped of everything, she has nothing upon which to depend for survival. Membership in the human community requires that others stand in solidarity with her in her grief and despair. It may be easy to do this when those who suffer are innocent of crime, but it becomes more complicated when they are guilty, as the city admits that she is. Still, human decency questions whether even the guilty should suffer alone, without the concern of others.

Perhaps the most troubling issue found in this poem is the city's resort to imprecation or cursing, the practice of calling down the wrath of God on another. Without condoning the practice, it is important to understand it. Cursing is a socially approved way that traditional societies have protected themselves against chaos. It is usually strictly controlled and never meant to be used casually or in private. It is a way of reestablishing order in society, not of avenging the wrong that one is made to endure. Its legitimacy is dependent on the worldview within which it is performed. There is significant biblical evidence showing that cursing was practiced in ancient Israel (see Josh 6:26). An example is found in the early tradition of the first promise made to Abram by God: "I will bless those who bless you, and the one who curses you I will curse" (Gen 12:3).

The contemporary worldview is significantly different from that of ancient Israel. Though it certainly does have to contend with chaotic situations, it does not conceive of order and chaos in the same way as did the ancients, and so it does not employ the same means to combat the latter in favor of the former. Cursing is not a way that modern societies use to restore order. Today most people in the West believe that social discord is caused by human beings. Therefore, this becomes an ethical issue and people look to human beings to restore social order.

COMMENTARY

LAMENTATIONS 2

THE DESTRUCTION OF THE CITY

THE WITNESS CRIES OUT: 2:1-19

Literary Analysis

Attention turns away from the city herself to God, the one responsible for the calamity that she has endured. Although the text does describe some of the tragic events, its primary focus is on the actions of God. The description of the horrors that gripped the city are some of the most graphic and disturbing of the entire Bible. What befell the city is beyond comparison; the catastrophe is "as vast as the sea" (v. 13). Mention of the day of God's unbridled wrath begins and ends the poem

(vv. 1c, 22b), forming a kind of frame that gives meaning to everything within it. This structuring makes clear that the day of God's terrifying wrath has dawned with the destruction of the city of Jerusalem.

The acrostic pattern of this poem is slightly different from that of the first poem. Here (and in chapters 3 and 4 as well) the seventeenth letter of the alphabet, precedes rather than follows the sixteenth letter. Most scholars believe that this difference reflects a time when the alphabet was not yet standardized. Structurally this second poem resembles the first in its three-line strophes, with the exception of verse 19, which has four lines. Finally, this poem is also in *qinah* meter. (See Introduction.)

This poem exhibits a very interesting feature. In all but five instances, a word or group of words appearing in one verse is repeated in the next, a second word or group connecting this second verse with the third, and so on, yielding a well-constructed literary unit. For example, verses 1 and 2 include the word "Lord," verses 2 and 3 have "Jacob," a reference to fire links verses 3 and 4, and a reference to enemy links verses 4 and 5. This literary technique binds together verses that may be otherwise quite distinct from each other.

The narrator speaks throughout most of the poem as one who had been an eyewitness to the disaster (vv. 1-19); Daughter Zion cries out only at the end (vv. 20-22). The narrator's words fall into two major sections: a description of the city's misfortunes (vv. 1-12) and an address to the city herself (vv. 13-19). A more detailed division seems appropriate: a listing of the acts of God that brought havoc upon the city (vv. 1-9a); a description of how God's destructive actions affected the lives of some of the inhabitants of the city (vv. 9b-12); a word of comfort (v. 13); a complaint against those who have turned against the city (vv. 14-16); an accusation against God (v. 17); a dirgelike cry urging Zion to cry out to the Lord (vv. 18-19). At the end, the city obeys the narrator's words and cries out in lament (vv. 20-22).

THE WRATH OF GOD: 2:1-9a

Exegetical Analysis

The poem opens with the same word as did the first poem: "Ah!" or "Ah how !" *('êkāh)*, the mournful cry traditionally associated with the dirge (v. 1). The wrath of God is mentioned twice in this first verse, underscoring the reason for the mournful cry. It is this divine wrath that brought about the suffering of the city. As noted earlier (1:12), the Hebrew word for "wrath" is the same as the word for "nostril." The image suggests intense anger that manifests itself in flared nostrils. The dirgelike character of these verses is also evident in the list of reversals of fortune that follows (vv. 1-3). In each instance the verb describes some form of collapse, with God as the instigator of each decline. In some of the verses, the general term "Lord" appears as a divine epithet (vv. 1, 2, 5, 7).

The narrator reports the details of the city's downfall primarily through the use of graphic verbs. The first verb appears only here in the entire Bible and for this reason the author's intent is uncertain. While the verb means "to obscure with clouds" or "to confuse," most commentators translate it as "humiliate" or "shame." As a consequence of the wrath of God, the city, the once cherished daughter Zion, suffers disgrace. The two images that follow reinforce this understanding: God has cast from heaven to earth the splendor of Israel and has disregarded this city that was once the footstool of the Lord. The first image is reminiscent of a scene with cosmic proportions, a scene that appears in two places within the prophetic writings. The great but sinful nations of Babylon (Isa 14:12) and Tyre (Ezek 28:14-17) are cast down from the high places which they once enjoyed to the very lowest places where they suffer disgrace. In a manner similar to the plight of these nations, Israel has experienced the same fate. Like a star falling from the sky, it has careened downward to humiliation and destruction.

The second image, the footstool, paints a picture of royalty. It suggests a throne room scene in which a sovereign being, either human or divine, is seated with feet firmly resting on a footstool.

Since various psalms characterize the temple as the footstool of God (see Pss 99:5; 132:7), there is some consensus among commentators that this is the meaning of the reference here as well. However the image is understood, this poem clearly implies that God has abandoned this privileged and sacred footstool

The extent of the destruction wrought by God unfolds. Verb upon verb conveys the horrors that the God who was once the city's patron protector now brings down upon her. God has swallowed up, broken down, and brought low (v. 2); cut down, withdrawn, and burned (v. 3); bent the bow, slain, and poured out fury (v. 4); become an enemy, swallowed up, and laid waste (v. 5); broken down, destroyed, ended, and spurned (v. 6); scorned, disowned, and delivered into the hands of enemies (v. 7); determined to ruin, allowed it to be swallowed up, caused mourning (v. 8); ruined and broke the bars of the city (v. 9a). Nothing was spared; no one escaped.

With three bold strokes of the brush, the narrator sketches the total sweep of the Lord's destructive force (v. 2). Although many translations suggest that the "habitations" or "dwellings" of Jacob refer to the homes of the people, the word is probably an allusion to the open pastures within which the flocks grazed. The Lord has swallowed them up without showing a trace of pity or mercy. The word used here for "mercy" comes from the word "to spare," and it denotes removing something from danger. Here it means that God swallows up without removing anyone or anything from danger.

While in some places the epithet Jacob would be an allusion to the northern tribes or the kingdom of Israel, here it is a poetic reference to the entire people of Israel. Besides swallowing up the open fields, God has also razed the fortified cities. Although Judah is actually the name of the southern region which contained the city of Zion, its juxtaposition with Jacob suggests that here it is another reference to the nation in its entirety. Finally, God has brought down to the ground in shame the kingdom itself with all of its officials. The word used for shame means "profane" or "defiled." In other words, not only is the nation destroyed, but it is also desecrated. Thus, God has destroyed the free and open spaces, the walled and protected cities, the holy nation itself.

In order to characterize the reversal of fortune that results in the nation's powerlessness, the narrator uses two metaphors that denote prowess (v. 3). The first metaphor is horn. Various ferocious animals are even more fearsome when they lower their heads and charge with their horns. However, they lose both their ferocity and often their bold spirit when their horns are broken off. This is the tenor or meaning of the metaphor "might" or "horn" of Israel. In anger, the Lord broke the horn of this formerly fierce nation, leaving it without defense and thus vulnerable to attack.

The second metaphor, hand, comes from the realm of military contest. The right hand is usually the hand that wields the weapon, whether it be used for protection or for aggression. God's right hand may have been raised in the nation's defense in the past (see Pss 10:12; 17:13-14; 89:13; and so on), but no more. The once protecting God did not ward off the enemies and so the people were vulnerable. These two metaphors suggest that God has deserted the nation, allowing its foes to attack it and triumph over it. In fact, it is God who has been the aggressor; it is God who has ravaged Jacob like fire that consumes everything in its path. In other words, God has first stripped the nation of its defenses, and then attacked it. The strophe begins and ends with the metaphor of fire. While fire is often an agent of purification, here it is the instrument of destruction. It is in blazing anger that God has broken Israel's horn of might and it is in consuming fire that God has swallowed up Jacob.

It is important to note some of the literary difficulties of the next verse (v. 4) before interpreting it. The primary problem is the question about the location of the phrase "like a foe." Placing it at the end of verse 4*a* makes that line disproportionately long and one of the remaining lines quite short. However, many commentators argue that, when it is the first word of verse 4*b*, it creates an awkward phrase. In order to remedy this difficulty, scholars have suggested various textual emendations, with corresponding translations. The lack of gender correspondence between one of the nouns and its verb creates a second difficulty. The Hebrew word for "right hand" is feminine in form, while its verb "set" is masculine. Some also remedy this discrepancy with an emendation, which explains the differences in various versions.

However one resolves these difficulties, the images contained within the verse continue the theme of God's destructive wrath. The implicit metaphor of God the warrior (v. 4a) is more fully developed here than it was in the previous verse, for the bow identifies the character of the divine warrior. The figure of a cosmic deity armed with bow and arrows is a common representation throughout ancient Near Eastern art. While such a depiction was usually associated with the mighty storm god, Israel often portrayed its God in this manner as well (see Pss 7:13; 77:17; 144:6). Here the Lord appears with the bow bent as if poised for an assault, a stance that a military archer might take. However, in this poem God is not defending Israel. Rather, God's powerful right hand holds the bow taut in the threatening stance of a foe.

Finally comes the terrible admission: the Lord has killed, has slaughtered (v. 4b). To this point in the poem divine wrath has been directed against open spaces and buildings. It has been figuratively described as casting down, or shaming, or weakening. The harsh reality of the situation is no longer masked. The people have been slaughtered, and it was the Lord who did the killing. There is no suggestion here that another is responsible for this annihilation. The bow was in God's divine hand; God is the one responsible for the slaying. And who are the victims? The poem states that they were those who brought delight, those in whom others took pride. These most cherished ones were the victims who fell by the hand of God. Their previous favored station makes the horror of their slaughter doubly felt.

Some read the phrase "in the tent of the daughter" with what precedes, while others read it with what follows. Associated with the preceding line, it would refer to the location where the slaughter took place. On the other hand, if, in order to resolve the irregularity in the length of the lines within this verse, the phrase is read with what follows, the focus would be on the divine wrath that accomplished the destruction. Whether the allusion is to specific killing or to total destruction, the fact that the desolation comes from the hand of God, the hand that in the past had been the source of protection, underscores the depth of the tragedy.

Earlier in the poem (v. 3) the narrator states that Lord has acted *in the presence* of the foe. Here (v. 5) as in the previous verse, the Lord actually acted *like* a foe. The word "swallow" appears twice in this line, emphasizing the all-encompassing nature of Israel's ruin. The image is one of total devastation. The crushed nation does not cling to some hope of restoration. Its enemy has devoured it, has swallowed it up; and that enemy was Israel's own God. The strongholds appear again (see v. 2), this time in parallel construction with palace or citadel:

he has destroyed (swallowed up)   all its palaces

he has laid in ruins   its strongholds

God has breached the defensive walls of fortification. This indicates the forcefulness of divine wrath. Israel had no protection. All that is left for the nation is grief. The narrator describes the intensity of this grief by means of alliteration, the use of two words that are not only similar in sound but in meaning: mourning *(taʾᵃniyāh)* and lamentation *(ʾᵃniyyāh)*. The narrator is also quite explicit in accusing God of being the cause of such anguish. The picture of desolate daughter Zion recalls the initial scene sketched in the first poem. There the city sat alone, weeping in the night (1:1-2). Here daughter Judah sits in the midst of her own destruction, mourning and lamenting.

Perhaps the most anguished blow against Zion was the ravaging and desecration of the temple (v. 4*c*). Israel considered this shrine the most hallowed spot on earth. It housed the Ark of the Covenant, the sacred object that served as Israel's palladium or standard in time of war. It held the tablets of the law received from God by Moses. Tradition claimed that it contained some of the manna from the wilderness along with the budding rod of Aaron (see Heb 9:4-5). More important, Israel cherished the Ark as the throne of God. It marked the spot where God was mysteriously present in the midst of the people in a unique and sacred way. The temple was itself holy, since King Solomon dedicated it for the worship of God (see 1 Kgs 8:1-13). Within it priests offered Israel's varied and elaborate sacrifices, and there the people celebrated its holy festivals. It was the center of the nation's religious life, and as such, it was the center of the universe. The people believed that the presence of God ensured its inviolability (see Jer 7:4). This poem shows how mistaken they were. It insists that it was Israel's own God who laid waste its sacred shrine (vv. 6-7).

Once again the narrator uses strong verbs to report the extent of the city's destruction: "broken down," "destroyed," "abolished" (v. 6). "Booth" stands in parallel construction with a word that means the sacred meeting place (cf. Josh 8:14):

he has broken   his booth   like a garden
he has destroyed   his sacred meeting place

"Booth" calls to mind the temporary huts that Israel set up in the fields and vineyards during times of harvest. These huts provided the harvesters the opportunity of remaining among their crops, guarding them from ruin or plunder. "Meeting place" is probably a reference to the tabernacle, an allusion to the tent of meeting in the wilderness (see Exodus 40; Leviticus 4; Numbers 4). It was the place where Moses consulted God in order to discover God's will for the people (see Exod 33:7). Both tabernacle and meeting place eventually came to be allusions to the temple. The parallel construction suggests that the booth is indeed the sacred meeting place, the temple. The poetry implies that God has dismantled the temple as if it were a temporary booth in a garden, a vineyard, or a field.

With the destruction of the temple, gone is the sacred place for meeting God, gone is the presence of God in the midst of the people, gone is the sanctuary with its altar of sacrifice. With the collapse of the temple, gone is the assurance of God's protection, gone is any sense of security against attack. Most horrifying is the thought that it was Israel's own God who perpetrated the desecration of this most sacred place. The very God who directed the nation to set this place apart from all other places, to consecrate it, and to preserve this consecration through the observance of a strict code of holiness, the God who descended from heaven to be with the people in this sacred place, has now broken it down and destroyed it.

Zion's destruction appears to know no bounds. Not only has God laid waste her hallowed structure, but the liturgical celebrations that took place within her confines have come to an abrupt end (v. 6b). No longer are weeks sanctified by the observance of the Sabbath, or months and years marked by the celebration of various feasts and festivals. Without its system of liturgical celebration the nation no longer enjoys the privilege of entering into the mysteries associated with sacred time. It no longer reenacts with God the events of creation or deliverance. The heavens are closed and the only time available to Israel is ordinary, conventional time. Its life has lost its sacred character.

God's anger or indignation is fierce, like a raging fire. In this fury God has spurned both king and priest. The priest's association with the temple and its system of worship and celebration is obvious. But what is the king's association? Most likely it is because it was King David who brought the ark of the covenant to the city of Jerusalem, placing it in the ceremonial tent that he had pitched for it. Then the king himself sacrificed burnt offerings and offerings of well-being before the LORD (see 2 Sam 1-19). It was another king, Solomon, who built the temple in Jerusalem, dedicating it to the Lord with prayer and sacrifice (see 1 Kings 8). The priests may have eventually assumed many of these ritual functions, but from the beginning the king's role in temple worship was firmly established. Now God spurns both sacred functionaries, the priests and kings alike.

God has scorned the altar (v. 7), which means that God has repudiated the sacrifices that priests would offer upon it. In other words, God has rejected the entire sacrificial system. God has disowned every aspect of the temple: the building itself, the worship that took place within it, the personnel who carried out the ritual actions, the sacred stone upon which the sacrifices were offered to God. Nothing is left. Even the most holy precincts of the temple, the sanctuary, has lost God's favor. God has abolished or ceased to care about (v. 6b), spurned (v. 6c), scorned and disowned (v. 7a) everything associated with the temple. Having broken it down and destroyed it, God has allowed Israel's enemies to enter this holy place, desecrating it by their presence. Mention of the walls of her palaces or citadels probably refers to the city rather than to the sanctuary (v. 5). Once

God had destroyed the walls of the city, the enemies had easy access to the ruins of the temple. There they raise a cry of celebration which is doubly bitter to hear. In the temple, the house of the LORD, where the Israelites themselves during times of festival once raised joyful celebration of God's goodness to the nation, their enemies now clamor exultantly over the temple's downfall.

Lest anyone think that all of this destruction happened because God was unable to stem the tide of enemy aggression, the text states that God carefully planned the demise of the city, measured out the dimensions of its walls for their destruction with the same precision as a builder might engage in preparing for construction or repair (v. 8). In this case, however, God's intent was demolition; ruin was Daughter Zion's destiny. The Hebrew creates a mixed metaphor. It states that the LORD did not withhold a destroying hand. However, the infinitive construct that ends the line (v. 8b) is a form of the verb "to swallow." Literally, the text states that God's hand did not refrain from swallowing. While most versions translate the verb to read "destroy," it is important to realize the nature of this destruction. It is a total and consuming rather than merely a crushing blow.

The technique of personification captures the poignancy of the situation. The city's wall and rampart, the defensive wall outside of the main city wall which gave the inner wall a degree of protection, both mourn (v. 8c). The image of a mourning wall suggests the comprehensiveness of the city's grief. It is surrounded, walled in by mourning, engulfed in sadness. In the ancient Near Eastern world, people did not lament in silence. The wailing was loud and often unrestrained. This characterization of grief appeals to both sight and sound. The enfeebled wall and rampart now keen like a mournful animal. Languish often refers to the extreme adversity experienced by those who are the objects of God's discipline or punishment (cf. Hos 4:3; Isa 33:9; Jer 14:2). All of this implies that the city suffers the consequence of its sins.

The poem states that the gates of this city have sunk into the ground as if fallen to their knees in defeat (v. 9a; cf. Ps 69:2). God has smashed the sturdy bars that reinforced them. There is no more protection. A city's final means of defense was its gate.

The main gate of a city was probably doubly fortified, consisting of an outer and an inner gate (see 2 Sam 18:24), built with more than one door. If the Solomonic gates of the great cities of Hazor, Gezer, and Megiddo boasted three or four doors, surely Zion was also elaborately constructed. The doors of the city gates generally consisted of wood, covered with metal and secured by bars of iron (see Ps 107:16; Isa 45:2). There might have been rooms for guards (see 2 Sam 18:24) and fortified towers that strengthened the city's defense (see 2 Chr 26:9). The city gate was also the area for social, administrative, and business transactions. The annihilation of the gate signaled the collapse of the city's defenses and the disintegration of any semblance of community life. The fury of divine wrath has swallowed the city and she has no recourse.

Theological and Ethical Analysis

One theological theme dominates this section (2:1-9a), namely the unrelenting ferocity of divine wrath. God seems to have unleashed this wrath mercilessly on the city and on the region surrounding it. Although some of the vocabulary used in the description of devastation suggests that Zion brought her fate down upon herself, one cannot help wondering whether or not the degree of its suffering was not excessive. Was God's anger merely retributive or could there have been vindictiveness in it as well? Did divine justice really demand such extreme measures? These are the kinds of questions that indescribable suffering raises in the minds of reflective people.

Unlike the contemporary scientific perception, in the ancient worldview, all dimensions of reality were somehow related and interdependent. It held that since everything was created by God and governed by divine law, whatever happened in one dimension of reality had repercussions on the others. Evidence of this thinking can be seen in the flood account, which states that all living things on earth suffer because of the sinfulness of humankind (see Gen 6:6-7, 11-12). In such a worldview, unbridled lawlessness posed a serious threat to the stability of the entire universe, and it had to be met by proportionate redress. The scope and character of Zion's downfall points to the heinousness of its previous sinfulness, unless, of course, God was deemed intemperate in punishing.

Theodicy refers to the human effort to understand and vindicate the justice of God in the face of evil in the world. Put another way, it addresses the question: How could a just God allow the innocent to suffer? While the desolation of Zion does not raise this theological and ethical issue in the same way as does the story of the innocent and steadfastly faithful Job, the comprehensiveness of the city's ruin makes one question the magnitude of God's reprisals. Does the punishment fit the crime? The narrator clearly states that God has swallowed up everything "without mercy" (v. 2), without removing anything from danger. There is no discrimination in God's chastisement. All suffer the same misfortune. One cannot help wondering: Is this fair? As has been the case throughout Lamentations, such questions are raised, but they are not answered. In a very real sense, the poems leave the answering to the reader.

Two other themes stand out in this section: God's apparent disinterest toward sacred institutions; and the role of the bystander in the face of the suffering of another. God is perceived as not only allowing Israel's enemies to tear down the religious shrine in Jerusalem and to bring its system of sacrifice and worship to an abrupt and tragic end, but actually engineering and executing the catastrophe. Israel may have thought that the sanctity of both the temple and its religious observances would save it from harm (cf. Jer 7:1-4), but the book of Lamentations shows quite another view. It explains that in God's eyes fidelity is more important than religious practice (cf. Ps 51:16-17; Isa 1:11; Jer 6:20). When such practice does not flow from fidelity, which seems to have happened in Israel all too easily, it is mere external observance and is unacceptable in God's eyes (see Amos 5:21).

The narrator appears to have been an eyewitness to Zion's downfall and to the anguish that she endures. At this point in the poem, this narrator simply reports what has happened, but does not in any way respond critically to what is observed. Various aspects of the city's affliction are reported in a manner that is neither judgmental nor sympathetic. The only hint of guilt on Zion's part, and it is merely a hint, is the word "languish" (v. 8c), which elsewhere describes the state of the nation after punishment by God (cf. Isa 33:9; Jer 14:2). One cannot help but wonder how anyone can stand dispassionately in the face of the anguish of another. Surely human solidarity would prompt one to some sense of compassion. Though such indifference is possible, is it morally acceptable?

THE ANGUISH OF THE PEOPLE: 2:9b-12

Exegetical Analysis

The narrator shifts the attention of his audience away from God's destructive campaign and toward some of the consequences that it effected in the lives of the people. He singles out various groups within the population. The first ones mentioned are civic leaders—the king and the other administrative officials. The Hebrew word that identifies these officials is sometimes translated "princes," but it can also more broadly include other civic leaders (1:6; 2:2). The poem states that these leaders are now in exile "among the nations." In the land of their exile the king and the leaders would be powerless. Furthermore, those people who survived the destruction of the city and its administrative structure would now be bereft of civic leadership. Anarchy usually ensues in cases such as this.

Added to this anarchy is the loss of religious direction (v. 9b). Though frequently translated "law" and denoting statutes and regulations, the Hebrew word *torah* really means "instruction" or "guidance." Despite the law's close association with Moses and the legal system of Israel, it was really the special domain of the priests. They were the ones to whom the people went for instruction in the law. With the demise of social and religious order, such instruction has now come to an end. This does not necessarily indicate that the priests are also in exile. Rather, it means that, with the destruction of the temple in which they performed their religious duties, the devotional rites which the priests celebrated there can no longer be performed. Consequently, the people would no longer gather there for priestly instruction.

A second religious practice has also ceased, namely, the revelatory visions of the prophets (v. 9c). Just as the priests were the agents who interpreted the law for the people, so the prophets were the ones through whom God delivered special knowledge of divine reality. It was through the priests and the prophets that God communicated with the people. Contrary to the people's false sense of security (cf. Jer 18:18), such communication has come to an end (cf. Ezek 7:26). The nation is now both politically and socially destabilized and religiously demoralized.

The narrator singles out another group within the population, namely the council of elders (v. 10). They were local leaders who participated in local government (cf. 1 Sam 8:4). Unlike the king and those leaders already mentioned (v. 9), they do not seem to have suffered forced exile. They remain behind to mourn the city's destruction, and they do so in a manner that was quite common in the ancient world. The very young and the very old were probably less a threat to the conquerors than those citizens who were in the prime of life and who held significant positions in the community. Therefore, children and the elderly were often left to fend for themselves when a city was captured or destroyed. However, the young and the old are probably linked here for poetic rather than historically descriptive reasons. Their juxtaposition creates a merism, a polar word-pair that represents the totality of what exists between the opposite poles. Both men (elders, v. 10a) and women (maidens, v. 10c) are left to mourn the destruction. Though the male-female pairing by itself encompasses the totality of the human race, elders-maidens includes everyone who by age falls somewhere in between these two generational poles. Though the poem only explicitly describes the elders and the maidens as mourning, the literary device (merism) suggests that the entire surviving population grieved.

The funeral rites in which the survivors participate are quite symbolic. The elders sit on the ground and the maidens bow their heads to it. They lower themselves to the ground in a sign of lowliness, acknowledging their fundamental humble condition (cf. 2 Sam 13:31). The elders sit in silence. Although loud wailing was a very common practice in such circumstances, there is also evidence that mourners often stood in silence in the face of unspeakable suffering (cf. Job 2:13). The elders also sprinkle dust on their heads (cf. Job 2:12) and clothe themselves in sackcloth (cf. Job 16:15). The dust is a reminder of human mortality (cf. Gen 3:19); the coarse sackcloth denotes mourning or repentance. All of these rites testify to aspects of human limitation that become so obvious and so burdensome in the presence of misfortune.

The plight of the innocent children unleashes the narrator's emotional response to the misery of the city (vv. 11-12). It is here that he identifies with its inhabitants. They are his people; he is one of them (v. 11). Although the destruction itself does not seem to have personally touched him, he is tormented nonetheless. The agony that he experiences in witnessing the plight of others invades every aspect of his being, and his body convulses in his distress. Using graphic imagery, he describes the physical effects of his inner anguish. His eyes are literally "shut up with tears." This could mean either that they are so filled that his sight is impaired and he cannot see, or that his weeping has been so intense and prolonged that he has no tears left to shed. Either meaning underscores the intensity of his grief.

In the first poem (1:20), Zion exclaimed that her stomach or innards were churning; the physical disturbance was violent. This same phrase, identifying the same profound inner agitation, describes an aspect of the narrator's misery as well (v. 11*a*). A second intestinal image continues the description of his inner turmoil; his liver is poured out on the ground (v. 11*b*). Since Israel believed that inner organs generally were the center of human emotion, the phrase vividly captures the narrator's inability to contain his intense emotional response to the horror that he has witnessed. He is overwhelmed by the ruin of the city (literally "the daughter of my people").

The particular aspect of this horror that has caused such a violent and uncontrollable reaction in him is the suffering borne by the most vulnerable of the population, the children. Two different words identify them (v. 11c). The first word refers to young children who have not yet reached puberty; the second, to those who are still suckling at their mothers' breasts. Sharp and unmistakable lines draw this picture of the pitiable condition of the children. They faint from lack of food (v. 11); they faint like the wounded who lie out in the open, whose life spirit is slowly fading away (v. 12). They naturally turn to their mothers who previously provided them with nourishment, but the mothers have nothing to give. Not only are their hands empty, but their breasts are as well. Their own lack of nourishment has caused their milk to dry up. Mothers clutch their children to their breasts, not to give them life, but to embrace them as they die. It is this heartbreaking scene that has torn the inner fabric of the narrator's being.

Theological and Ethical Analysis

It is not just suffering, but the suffering of the innocent that seizes the narrator and wracks his being (2:9b-12). Such suffering often throws several firmly held theological principles into question. The most obvious one is the theory of retribution which holds that reward will come to those who are good, while wickedness will be punished. This theory functions not only as the standard for justice, both present and future, but as a basis upon which people try to structure society. The claim is that this is the way God made the world to work. At least that seems to have been the thinking of many people in the past, and it continues to be the expectation of many today.

Covenant theology provides an added dimension to the theological theme of retribution, that of corporate involvement. Israel believed that God had entered into covenant with the entire nation (see Deut 7:6), not merely with its leaders or its able-bodied men. Therefore, the rewards promised and the punishments threatened applied to the entire population—the young and the old, those who transgressed the covenant ordinances and those who were faithful to them. As distasteful as this notion may appear to be to Western understanding of justice, the fact remains that the corporate nature of the covenant carried with it communal responsibility and communally endured consequences.

Still, the suffering of the innocent poses several questions: If, as the religious tradition insists, God did indeed create an ordered world (see Genesis 1), why does God allow situations of injustice to arise and to hold sway? Is God unjust? disinterested? capricious? Such questions raise the issue of theodicy, an issue discussed above. Considered another way, innocent suffering challenges the idea of the universal governing power of God. It suggests that God may indeed be just but not powerful enough to hold back the flood of injustice that seems at times to take over the world.

Divine justice and divine omnipotence appear to be constantly on trial. This is especially true in the face of human holocaust, whether this holocaust be: the "final solution" enacted by the Nazis; the enslavement and slaughter of indigenous people at the time of the colonization of Africa, Central and South America, or the conquest of the frontier of the United States. The destruction of entire populations continues into our own day with the ethnic cleansing that is practiced in so many places in the contemporary world. The same theological questions are raised today: How can a just God allow this to happen? Is it possible that God is powerless to prevent it?

There is another way of dealing with the issue of innocent suffering, a way that may be theologically acceptable, but no more anthropologically satisfying. It is to question the usefulness of the theory of retribution rather than the goodness or power of God. Human life and human history both demonstrate that the good do not always enjoy reward nor do the wicked always suffer punishment. The innocent do in fact suffer and unprincipled people frequently live prosperous and satisfying lives. In this poem the innocent are indeed caught up in the just punishment of the wicked. While the theory of retribution may be a useful way of understanding some, perhaps even most, situations in life, it is still inadequate to explain all of them. It collapses in the face of innocent suffering. It appears that neither God nor the theory of retribution offers a satisfying explanation of this innocent suffering.

When confronted with such unanswered questions, the biblical tradition offers the example of Job, who in the end acknowledged the incomprehensibility of his dilemma and placed his fate in the hands of the mysterious God (Job 42:1-6). This is the stance of faith, that holds steadfastly to belief in God's ultimate covenant fidelity. It is the stance of hope, that trusts that God will not desert the people in their time of need. For those who witness the suffering of others, it is the stance of solidarity, that enters empathetically into their misfortune. The inability to understand the suffering of the innocent is a constant reminder of both the vulnerability and the limitation of the human condition, a condition in which humans stand needy and humbly before God and in need of the unselfish support of others.

ZION IS ADDRESSED: 2:13-19

Exegetical Analysis

The narrator moves from bemoaning the sufferings endured by Jerusalem to speaking directly to the city. Translators are challenged by the first two lines of the first strophe of this section (v. 13*ab*). They contain three phrases, all introduced by the same interrogative: What can I testify to? What can I compare you to? What can I make like you? Most commentators believe that the three verbs in these phrases are synonymous and the repetition of thought emphasizes the incomparability of the city's misery. Thus the questions are rhetorical. What can be said about it, or testified in its favor? Nothing. To what can it be compared? Nothing. To what can it be likened? Nothing. There is no way to console the city, identified here as Daughter Jerusalem/ Daughter Zion. The use of the metaphor "sea" in the final line of the strophe supports this view. While many features of the sea lend themselves to a characterization of the city's ruin, the text concentrates on its vastness or immeasurability. There is no standard that can measure Israel's devastation. It is too vast. The wound that the city has sustained will not be healed.

The narrator next mentions three groups of people who intensify Zion's sufferings: the city's own false prophets; outsiders who taunt her as she sits defeated in the midst of her own wreckage; and her enemies who rejoice at her ruin (vv.14-15). The most despicable are the prophets (v. 14). They were the messengers of God, privileged to deliver God's word to the people. They were the conscience of the nation, entrusted with the task of calling the people to their covenant obligations. The narrator does not exonerate the city of its culpability, but he does accuse the prophets of proclaiming messages that were false and that covered this culpability like whitewash covers decay. Had the prophets been faithful to their charge and called the people to repentance, the people might have reformed their lives and thus escaped the wrath of God. As it was, the false oracles merely confirmed the people in their sinfulness.

The city herself had earlier called upon all of the passersby to turn their attention to her and to consider whether or not there was any sorrow to compare with hers (1:12). The narrator states that these passersby do indeed look upon the city, but not with compassion. Instead, they taunt her with both words and actions (v. 15). Here clapping hands is not meant as applause. It is a form of mockery, as are hissing and the wagging of heads. In her distress, Zion looks for sympathy and she receives ridicule. Insult is added to injury. Titles of honor that previously praised her privileged status now turn against her in derision. In the past she reveled in her glorious titles: "the perfection of beauty" (Ps 50:2), "the joy of all the earth" (Ps 48:2). The first expression reflects the former splendor of the city; the second suggests that Zion was the medium through which God showered blessings on all the earth. The passersby who mock her throw these epithets in her face. Is this ravaged city the one who had been so favored in the past? Now she is anything but beautiful, and no one rejoices in her.

The enemies too take delight in the city's plight (v. 16). They jeer her. Like the passersby, they hiss at her. Although the gnashing of teeth is frequently associated with the expression of profound grief (see Matt 22:13; Luke 13:28), the Hebrew word suggests anger directed against another (cf. Job 16:9; Pss 35:16; 37:12; 112:10). If casual passersby deride the city, what can be expected of her enemies? They not only take pleasure in the calamity that has struck her down, they even take credit for it. They claim to have swallowed her up. Although they do not identify the day for which they had longed as the eschatological Day of the LORD, this long anticipated day certainly must have been in the background for both the city and the narrator. How tragically ironic! Traditionally, Israel looked to this Day as a time when God's judgment would fall upon its enemies. However, the reverse is true. It is the enemies who have longed for the Day and who now rejoice at its dawning.

The narrator sums up his portrayal of the tribulations of the city (v. 17) by returning to several themes developed earlier in the poem. He begins by reiterating what may be the most painful statement of all: Zion's ruin, the agony of her inhabitants, and the derision that she has endured because of it have all been the doing of the LORD. This destruction was not the result of some sudden impulse; God's wrath did not flare up capriciously. God carefully planned it (v. 8). In fact, God seems to have determined it long ago (literally: in days of antiquity). This is probably a reference to the covenantal pact freely entered into by both God and the people at the very beginning of the nation's existence. At that time, the people agreed to abide by God's ordinances and to accept the penalty for disloyalty. God promised to guide and protect the people, but also reserved the right to punish them if they turned away from their obligations. It was the sinfulness of the city that set this ancient plan in motion.

The destruction by God is total. There is nothing to pity; nothing is spared (v. 2). Having demolished the city, God allowed Zion's foes to rejoice over her misfortune cf. (v. 16). God turned upside down the favoritism once shown to this glorious city by breaking the horn or might of Israel (v. 3) and exalting the horn or might of Israel's enemies.

The narrator brings to a conclusion the heartrending description of Zion's ordeal, and he exhorts the city to turn to God in supplication (vv. 18-19). The Hebrew text poses several problems for interpreters. The literal translation of the first half-line (v. 18a) is: "Their heart (singular) cried to the Lord." To whom does "their" refer? Certainly not the prophets, passersby, or enemies just described. Most likely "they" are the inhabitants of the city. Some commentators maintain that here, as was the case earlier in the poem (vv. 1-12), the narrator is addressing the reader. However, the rest of the strophe is clearly directed to the city. It seems unnecessary for the narrator to turn to the reader at this time. Consequently, most translations emend the half-line to read: Cry aloud to the Lord. This emendation fits well the sense of the rest of the narrator's words, which consist of a series of imperatives: Cry aloud; shed tears; give yourself no rest; arise; cry out; pour out your heart; lift up your hands!

The meaning of "wall of Daughter Zion" in the second half-line (v. 18a) presents another difficulty. Most commentators consider this an example of synecdoche, a figure of speech in which a part (the wall) is used for the whole (the city). In this rendering, the phrase would function as direct address: Cry out to the Lord, Zion. The narrator exhorts the city to beseech the Lord with tears and supplications, to weep copiously (like a torrent) and constantly (day and night), in a characteristically dirgelike manner. There is to be no rest. This may appear to be an unnecessary exhortation, since from the outset the city is seen weeping (vv. 1:2, 16; 2:5). However, here the narrator tells her to join her tears with prayers, particularly night prayers. Furthermore, they are to be prayers of supplication, not merely of desolation, as would be the case in a dirge. The time of night was generally divided into three four-hour watches. The narrator exhorts the city to rise at the beginning of each of these watches in order to pour out her heart to the Lord. Since its destruction would have made such watches pointless, the narrator most likely uses this reference to encourage persistent, even unrelenting, entreaty. Finally, the narrator directs the city to lift up her hands in the traditional gesture of prayer and to allow the sentiments of her heart to pour out freely like water flowing from its source.

Zion has reason for tears and need of prayer. The life of her children is in jeopardy. The fourth line of this unusually long strophe (v. 19) describes again the unspeakable distress of the most vulnerable of the inhabitants. Children are out in the open, fainting from hunger (vv. 11-12). This is the second time in the poem that the narrator concentrates on their plight, evidence that its tragedy has pierced his own heart. It may be that he believes that as he has been moved by their innocent suffering, so will God be moved. In this spirit he counsels Zion to turn her maternal instincts into prayers for their survival.

Throughout this address, the narrator has turned compassionate eyes and a caring heart to the beleaguered city. He is not unconcerned, uninvolved. He seeks to comfort, but does not know what to do. He might point an accusing finger toward others, but what consolation will this bring? There is only one recourse, and that is God.

Theological and Ethical Analysis

The role played by the prophets is an unenviable one. Chosen by God, they deliver the divine word to God's people. Such was the case with the prophets described in this poem (2:13-19). Because they were mediators between God and the community, they were considered holy people and they often enjoyed the privileges that accompanied such an honor. It was their responsibility to call the people to fidelity to their covenant commitment. This responsibility was not burdensome when the people were faithful. However, when the prophets challenged their behavior, the people often turned against them (cf. Jer 38:6).

Religious leadership of itself may not be prophetic. The history of Israel recounts stories of leaders who were primarily administrators, directing the activities of the community and managing its goods (cf. 2 Sam 8:15-18). Other leaders carry out priestly duties, offering sacrifices and leading the community in prayer (cf. Lev 9:1-24). There are also professional teachers and healers, all in some way acting in the role of leader (cf. Exod 18:13-23). Though not strictly speaking prophetic, such responsibilities can be fulfilled in a manner that is certainly prophetic.

The biblical tradition suggests that the prophet is one who has an unusually clear insight into the contemporary challenges of the covenant commitment and proclaims the implications of this insight (cf. Amos, chapters 1 and 2). Depending upon their own attitudes, those who hear the prophetic word will either appreciate and heed the prophet's admonitions or disregard and resent them. When the prophetic message consoles or energizes the people, they are inclined to honor the prophets. However, when it challenges or condemns them, the people often reject, denounce, persecute the prophets, even put them to death in order to silence the prophetic voice (cf. Jer 37:11-16). It takes great courage to speak the truth as one sees it, a courage that not everyone seems to possess.

Now as then, religious leadership may require, even necessitate, prophetic insight. Similar theological and ethical issues surface. The administrators who direct the activities of the members of the community may sometimes have to redirect those activities and risk incurring the displeasure of the members. Those who manage the goods of the community may be torn between methods that will ensure the community's financial benefit and survival and issues of social justice. Leaders of prayer may discover that raising the social consciousness of the people actually enrages them. Teachers and healers may also be called to take unpopular stands in the community. Taking a stand for truth as one sees it can be as perilous today as it was for Israel's prophets. It requires both integrity and courage.

On the other hand, there are those in positions of leadership who are not faithful to their charge. There are those who reassure when they should question, who support when they should challenge. There are those who side with the ruling powers, who enjoy the privilege and power that religious leadership can give. They are like the false prophets decried in this poem, who sought to protect the status quo, who failed to expose Zion's infidelity. Such prophets fail in their responsibility to God, to the community, and to truth.

LORD, LOOK WHAT YOU HAVE DONE: 2:20-22

Exegetical Analysis

In the final verses of this poem (vv. 20-22), Zion follows the narrator's admonition and turns to the LORD. However, she does not turn in supplication as the narrator counseled her to do. There is no confession of sin here, nor is there a cry for relief. Her prayer is indirect; she asks the LORD to look and to see (1:11), to consider who the victims of such horrible suffering actually are. Some commentators believe that this is a veiled reference to Israel's status as a chosen people. While there is nothing explicit in the text to support this conjecture, such a suggestion is certainly not out of place. What follows the city's plea is the mention of a string of people whom the enemy have slaughtered: children, priests and prophets, the young and the old. All have been swallowed up.

The first scene that the city addresses (v. 20) is perhaps one of the most gruesome in the entire Bible. Women have been reduced to such desperate straits that they have not only watched helplessly as the children to whom they gave birth starve to death, but facing the same starvation themselves they have been driven to cannibalism, eating the dead bodies of these very children (cf. Deut 28:53-57). Behavior that is truly appalling compounds this loss of innocent life. To what depths of degradation have these people fallen! Not only have they violated the most intimate bonds of human life, but they have desecrated the hallowed precincts of the sanctuary. The priests and prophets lose their lives in the very place where they carried out their sacred duties. The streets are strewn with bodies of the young and old alike. The death of the children and the youth is particularly traumatic, for it shuts off the possibility of future generations. They are the hope of the future, and now that hope has been destroyed.

The final scene is both tragic and accusatory. Zion parallels her deplorable circumstances to the celebration of a religious festival. While this is a kind of comparison, for Zion it is also a lamentable reversal. Previously the LORD had summoned Zion to the festivities; now those who gather to celebrate are her enemies, whom she considers "terrors all around" (cf. Jer 6:25; 20:3, 10; 46:5; 49:29). In former times, the day of celebration was a religious festival, now it is the Day of the LORD's wrath. Finally, the prescribed victim for the sacrifice offered during the festival was a bull, a lamb, or a goat; now it is the population of the besieged city.

The poem ends on a note of desperation. No one has survived; no one has been spared. The city lovingly refers to her citizens as children, those she has fondled and cradled in her arms and those she has reared. They are all gone, swallowed up by her enemies. Although outsiders may have conquered the city and butchered her inhabitants, Zion contends that it was actually the LORD who did this; the LORD was her real enemy.

The city has described the extremities of her circumstances. But why does she do this? She is accusing God of perpetrating these horrors. What does she hope to gain? Is she trying to shame God? Does she think that the God who has so inflicted her without pity will relent and eventually show compassion? The text leaves the reader with these unanswered questions.

Theological and Ethical Analysis

Zion's prayer is an accusation against God: Look at what you have done! See to whom you have done it! (2:20-22). This should not be seen as a form of blasphemy. Rather, such accusation is a constitutive part of the prayer of lament (cf. Pss 22:1; 42:9; 88:14). In its own way, it is an admission of human limitation. Those who suffer cry out to another because there is nothing that they can do to relieve their own agony. Furthermore, directing the lament to God is an acknowledgment of God's power over the circumstances of life. It also suggests some degree of confidence that God will do something to remedy a situation that is beyond human control. The lament is a prayer of deep and humble faith. In fact, the lament is the largest category of psalms in the Bible, including over forty individual complaints and a dozen or more national or communal complaints.

This poem addresses another important issue, the disposition of dead bodies and the mention of cannibalism. Even in natural disasters and in war, judicious attention is given to the care of bodies. In fact, the way a culture understands the nature of the human person is reflected in its funeral and burial customs. Whether these customs are elaborate or relatively simple, they demonstrate reverence for the corpse. Many ancient cultures required funeral rites if the deceased was to enjoy existence in an afterlife. The body is accorded respect because it previously participated in the integrity of the individual person's life on earth. Conversely, desecration of the body was and continues to be a way of dishonoring the person. Perhaps the ultimate humiliation is the cannibalization of the human body, a practice that most people find repulsive. Although throughout history there have been tribes that ate parts of their enemies, thinking that in this way they might gain the strength or courage or wisdom of those enemies, most people consider eating the flesh of another human being a violation of nature itself.

As reprehensible as cannibalism may be, in certain situations it raises complex ethical questions. The circumstances sketched in this poem are a case in point. In the devastated city, starvation was not merely a possibility; it was a reality. Some of the children succumbed to its ravages. With no other source of nourishment, mothers, in order to survive, were forced to eat the fruit of their own wombs. Even if the scene is symbolic, it is particularly abhorrent, because it is not merely people feeding on human flesh, but mothers eating the bodies of their own dead children. The circumstances present a dilemma that is not an easy one to resolve. On the one hand is the respect due the remains of a once live human being; on the other hand is the survival of another. Were the women described in the poem wrong in what they did? Today some ethicists would say yes; others would say no. As repugnant as this may have been, the mothers' intent was not to dishonor their children, but to preserve their own lives. Such a situation is, in any event, a tragic example of ultimate desperation and horrendous humiliation for both the mothers and the entire people. Earlier in the tradition such appalling behavior is listed as one of the curses that will descend upon the people if they are unfaithful to their covenant commitment (see Deut 28:53).

COMMENTARY

LAMENTATIONS 3

THE STRONG MAN'S LAMENT

Literary Analysis

The third poem has some features in common with the first two poems. It follows the acrostic pattern, having three lines to each strophe. However, it is a more elaborate poetic composition: each of the three lines begins with the same successive letter of the alphabet. As was seen in the second poem, this one contains a noticeable repetition of words and grammatical forms. Perhaps the most striking difference is the dramatic shift in perspective. While two voices (a narrator and Daughter Zion) spoke in the first poems, a third voice is heard here. Sometimes it is the voice of one man alone, at other times it is a collective voice as if one person is speaking in the name of the entire community. The traditional view has presumed that this man is the suffering prophet Jeremiah. However, within the recent past commentators have identified him variously as King Josiah, King Jehoiachin, or King Zedekiah. Because there is no definitive identification in the text itself, other commentators consider this mysterious speaker as either an anonymous typical sufferer or as a representation of the entire suffering people. Finally, the movement from singular speaker to plural has led some to view him as a kind of fluid personality, sometimes an individual and sometimes the community.

The poem does not easily fall into recognizable literary units, leading commentators to suggest various divisions. Obvious literary units do not always follow the acrostic pattern. For example, verses 1-20 consist of a complaint and verses 21-25 are an expression of hope. While these verses manifest elements of an individual lament, separating verses 20 and 21 interrupts the three-line acrostic unit (vv. 19-21). The following division is a way of understanding the literary structure of the poem: 1-20, individual lament; 21-24, expression of hope; 25-39, instruction on the way divine justice functions in the lives of women and men; 40-47, communal exhortation and complaint; 48-57, a second individual lament with a plea for help; 58-66, a prayer for vengeance.

I Am the Man: 3:1-20

Exegetical Analysis

In contrast to the first poems that depict the suffering as that of a woman, this chapter presents it as the experience of a man who is not merely describing what happened to others, but who is reporting his own plight. Furthermore, this is not just any kind of a man. He is a strong man; the Hebrew suggests that he might even be a soldier. The contrast between the implications intended by this designation and the description that follows is striking. The one whose responsibility it was to protect the vulnerable members of society is himself the victim of disaster. The emphatic form of the first-person pronoun underscores this: *I am the strong man! I am the one who has endured all of this! I am the one who has become a contradiction!* The affliction that this man has experienced is characterized as fierce wrath, the kind of wrath that burns, overflows, and sweeps away everything before it.

Though this unit contains features of an individual lament, the strong man does not direct his words to God, as is customary in this particular literary genre. Rather, his accusation against his persecutor takes the form of a description directed to an anonymous audience. He heaps complaint upon complaint (vv. 2-17a), reporting how he has been overwhelmed by the burning wrath of his assailant. Compounding word picture with word picture, he creates a kind of collage of horror. Although the enemy is not named, the pronominal subject of all of the verbs that follow suggests that, throughout this series of accusation, the enemy is one and the same. This enemy has driven the strong man, as a shepherd or herder might drive a flock, not into green pastures (cf. Ps 23:2-3) but into darkness, to a place where there is no light (v. 2). The strong man claims that the wrath that he endures is both restrictive and unrelenting. Only he has been made to endure the torturous hand of this adversary, and he has had to endure it "again and again, all day long" (v. 3).

The physical damage inflicted by the continual punishment meted out by the enemy's hand has left the man's entire body an open wound: flesh, skin, and bones are racked and broken (v. 4). Some commentators have translated the verb as "waste away," suggesting dramatic loss of weight resulting from unrelenting hunger. Others take their cue from the mention of broken bones and contend that the damage done resulted from a violent assault that, while battering the flesh, would break the skin as well as the bones. Other imagery reinforces the military connotations associated with the idea of strong man. "Besieged and enveloped" (v. 5) is military vocabulary suggesting attack and confinement. However, this seems to be figurative language, for the man says that he was encircled with bitterness and tribulation. The word translated "bitterness" or "misery" is also rendered "gall" (cf. Ps 69:21), a bitter product of a plant which became synonymous with poison.

The darkness of death (v. 6) is the ultimate affliction. This place of darkness resembles the primal darkness of chaos and those who enter that place return to an existence that is really no existence at all. This is the second time that the strong man has accused his attacker of forcing him into darkness (v. 2), an example of the poet's weaving themes from one verse to another. The association with the dead suggests finality; there is no return from the misery into which the strong man has been plunged.

The idea of confinement continues (vv. 7-9). The strong man is walled in and weighed down with heavy fetters (v. 7). Many persecutors even today torture their victims in this way, confining them with chains in a very small space. This not only exaggerates their inability to move around, but it can also leave them with the sensation that the walls are actually moving in on them, threatening to crush them in the process. So confined, the strong man cries out in prayer for help (v. 8). The intensity of his plea is evident in his use of two separate verbs, both of which mean cry for help. The confinement that his enemy has forced upon him not only keeps him in, but also prevents his prayer from reaching its destination. He is shut in; his prayer is shut out.

Indication that these descriptions are meant to be taken metaphorically is evident in the next line (v. 9). The idea of confinement is continued through the use of the image of a wall constructed of hewn stones. However, this is not a wall that confines the man. Instead, it prevents him from following a straight path. If he were truly chained he would not be able to move in any direction. This disparity in the metaphors suggests that the strong man is probably imprisoned not in some dank dungeon, but rather in his own affliction and helplessness. The rod of wrath of which he spoke in the beginning of his lament (v. 1) has beaten him down, cast him into darkness and confined him there with no hope of escape. The metaphors in the next section confirm this interpretation.

The previous line's mention of "ways" and "paths" becomes the bridge to the next set of metaphors. The strong man continues his complaint against the treatment that he endures at the hand of his foe, joining images of imprisonment to those of ferocious animals (v. 10). He characterizes his enemy first as a bear and then as a lion. The meaning of the metaphors is obvious. Both animals lie in wait for the unsuspecting and vulnerable man, as if he were their prey. They are ready to pounce on him when he is least expecting it. He is no match for their cunning or their prowess. Like these fierce animals, his adversary has attacked him, has dragged him off the path, mauled him, and left him desolate (v. 11). This enemy is brutal and life-threatening. There is a shift in imagery in the next line (v. 12). Here the man depicts his enemy as an archer and himself as prey, as a hunted animal. Whether the man is the prey of fierce animals or of a hunter, the sense is the same. He is the vulnerable target and his enemy is the fearsome stalker.

The hunting image introduced above continues to unfold (v. 13). The archer's aim is accurate and the arrows from his quiver (poetically identified as "sons of the quiver") penetrate the strong man's innards. Though frequently translated as "heart," the word is really "kidneys." The various nuances that this word yields underscore the significance of the metaphor. First, the kidneys are in the interior of the body. To be struck there indicates that the blow was quite deep. Second, kidneys were thought to be one of the centers of life and, and if he was struck there, the strong man would have sustained a life-threatening blow. Third, kidneys were frequently considered the seat of emotion and, therefore, such piercing would be an assault on more than the man's physical integrity. Finally, one could only be struck in the kidneys from behind. This suggests that the hunted man was either unaware of the jeopardy in which he stood or he was hit while trying to escape. In either case, such an attack would have been cowardly.

The last two lines of this strophe (vv. 14-15) recount some of the consequences of this relentless attack. The strong man has become a laughingstock. The Hebrew is uncertain here. It suggests that the man is shamed either before all people or specifically before all of his own people. Because of a later identification with his own people, most commentators believe that here the reference is to all people generally. As a result of the tribulations that cast him down, this man is no longer respected ("I have become the laughingstock"). In fact, he is the object of the ridicule of others (cf. Jer 20:7), the subject of their taunting songs. Such torment never stops; it continues all day long (v. 14). In many societies the loss of honor is sometimes a greater affliction than the misfortune that caused it. Some people have actually taken their own lives rather than live without honor. Here the strong man's persecutor has first shamed him and then filled him with bitterness and wormwood (v. 15). Like gall (see v. 5), wormwood is a bitter herb. The poem states that the strong man has not only tasted them, but he has been sated with their bitterness. One might say that just as he consumed them, so their bitterness consumed him.

The humiliation of the strong man continues (v. 16). His attacker seems to have pushed his face down into the dirt, grinding his teeth into the gravel. His humiliation is compounded when he is made to cower in the ashes. Because ashes are the remnants of burning, they carried the connotation of worthlessness. They signified misery, and people sprinkled them upon their heads as a sign of repentance, mourning, and humiliation. To cower in the ashes would be an indication of extraordinary disgrace.

In a simple statement, the strong man sums up his plight: "My soul is bereft of peace" (v. 17a). The Hebrew word that is frequently translated as "soul" is a form of the verb "to breathe" and, therefore, it is also rendered as "breath" or "life" (v. 17a). It designates the person's life force. The verb translated "bereft" carries the basic meaning of strong disapproval and, therefore, rejection. The man's soul, his life force, every aspect of his being, has been denied even a glimmering of peace, the kind of peace that includes security, health, and prosperity. This stricken man is deprived of all of the good things that life has to offer.

The focus of the complaint shifts from the assaults of the enemy to the devastation that they wrought in the life of the strong man (vv. 17b-20), who has forgotten what happiness is: "Gone is my glory" (v. 18). The word that some translate as "glory" might be better rendered as "endurance." It probably functions as a part of a hendiadys, a figure of speech in which two words connected by a conjunction express one idea. The second word of the pair is "hope" or "expectation." Together they might mean "enduring expectation." Thus, whatever endurance or hope in the LORD the man may have clung to in the past is now shattered.

Throughout this list of accusations the strong man has never identified his enemy. For the first time in this poem, this enemy is explicitly named. It is the LORD (v. 18). It was God who assaulted the strong man and brought him down; it was God who walled him in and tortured him; it was God who attacked him in the manner of a savage animal. It is no wonder that the man has lost hope in the LORD. Remembering such affliction and the restlessness that it precipitates was as bitter to him as are wormwood (v. 15) and gall (v. 5).

The meaning of verse 20 is the subject of extensive scholarly discussion. The Masoretic or ancient Hebrew Text contained emendations known as "corrections of the scribes." They were slight emendations of a text which expresses something considered inconsistent with the majesty of God. This was usually some form of excessive anthropomorphism, an attribution to God of some human characteristic. Some commentators allege that there was an emendation of verse 20 in an early version of the text. Contemporary versions render this verse in a way similar to the following: Remembering this affliction and misery, this wormwood and gall, my soul or life force is brought low within me. Those who believe that there was a correction, suggest that originally it was God's soul that was brought low. At issue is not the concept that God might grieve, for God's emotional response is found in many places in the Bible. What might be considered excessive here is the attribution of a soul or life force to God. If this was indeed the original reading, it is clear why some scrupulous scribe might emend the text, for it would be depicting God in a way that is far too anthropomorphic for some. What is interesting about this discussion is less the exact reading of the text than the idea that scribes would consider it their duty to uphold God's dignity.

Although the first twenty verses of this poem constitute a series of complaints in the nature of lamentation, they contain no specific details that might identify the one who is suffering. Nor are they descriptive of actual historical events. Furthermore, they are all figurative characterizations of the suffering of an individual rather than the tribulations endured by a city or a nation. Even if this man represents the entire population, here we are looking deeply into the suffering of a person who, though once considered strong, is now quite vulnerable and overwhelmed by adversity.

Theological and Ethical Analysis

Anyone who has suffered can identify with the sentiments expressed by this tormented individual (3:1-20). The dramatic figures of speech and the metaphorical imagery together fashion an account that possesses broad applicability. Woven throughout this tapestry is a characterization of God that is bound to offend the religious sensibilities of some. The issue here is not that of a retributive God, one who strictly punishes the wicked for their offenses. Nor is it theodicy, the defense of divine righteousness in the face of innocent suffering. Rather, it is of divine brutality, an image of God that finds its parallel in the book of Job (see Job 6:4; 19:6-12).

While it may appear that such an image of God is theological in origin, more than likely an anthropological presupposition is at work in fashioning such a view. According to the theory of retribution, goodness is rewarded with happiness and prosperity while wickedness is punished with misfortune. Therefore, God turns retributive when human beings are sinful. When human unrighteousness can be identified, God is thought to be just even while inflicting punishment. However, when misfortune cannot be traced back to any human transgression, God is perceived as being brutally capricious. In either case, it is the anthropocentric or human-centered point of view that characterizes God as the perpetrator of the misfortune.

Such a characterization of human cause and divine response may correspond to a traditional worldview, but it is not compatible with a more modern perspective. Today people realize that much human suffering originates from some form of human vulnerability, whether physical, emotional, or spiritual. All people are subject to pain and illness, to uncertainty and fear. They are plagued with ambiguity and misunderstanding, and they can become the victims of the cruelty of others. To question why God has afflicted them in such ways or allowed others to so afflict them presumes that the order of the universe is structured according to anthropocentric principles, that the universe itself functions to reward or punish human beings.

People today realize that anthropocentric concerns do not determine the workings of the universe. In fact, the rest of the natural world appears to be unconcerned about human aspirations. Despite the popularity of the "anthropic principle," which claims that evolutionary development was always directed toward the ultimate appearance of the human species, many scientists still insist that the universe itself is indifferent to humanity as such. Although some form of retribution is still part of the thinking of many people, scientific and technological advances call for a reconfiguration of this kind of worldview. Such a reconfiguration will not necessarily provide an explanation of human suffering. Rather, it may pose entirely different questions. For example, one might ask: Why did God create a world so filled with danger and ambiguity? Why did God make human beings so incomplete, so vulnerable, so susceptible to suffering? While the reader might raise such questions, the book of Lamentations does not. It simply describes human suffering, suffering that cries out in agony and complaint, suffering that seeks an ear that is open to hear and an eye that is willing to see.

I HAVE HOPE: 3:21-24

Exegetical Analysis

The strong man's complaint moves into expressions of hope. Both the literary structure and the content of this short passage

(vv. 21-24) focus attention on this theme. The phrase, "There I have hope" frames the passage in a circular fashion (vv. 21, 24). The grounds for this hope are then stated within the frame (vv. 22-24). The placement of this expression of hope has caused significant scholarly dispute regarding its meaning. Throughout the first part of the poem (vv. 1-20), the strong man has consistently cried out in complaint because of the agonizing misfortunes that he has been forced to endure. This present expression of hope radically shifts his sentiments. Some claim that such a shift is common in prayers of lament where complaint is often followed immediately by a declaration of trust. Others maintain that the phrase "call to mind" (v. 21) continues the thought of the previous two verses of the acrostic group (vv. 19-20) to which verse 21 belongs. They would emend those verses to suggest that it is God who remembers and who is brought low (see above regarding v. 20 and the "corrections of the scribes"). According to this emended reading, such divine behavior would instill hope in the strong man. However, since sentiments of hope are commonplace in laments, such emendation is not deemed necessary here.

A second feature in this verse has also puzzled commentators. The word "therefore" normally refers to what preceded it. In this case ("therefore I have hope," v. 21), that would mean that the strong man's hope issues from the torment against which he has been railing. One need not resort to the emendation described above if "therefore" is regarded as part of the frame surrounding the reasons for the strong man's hope. In this way it functions less in a linear manner than in poetic fashion.

The word for "hope" means both "waiting" and "confidence." Here the strong man is waiting for something. True, he would not be waiting if he did not have confidence in that for which he waited, but here the primary focus is on the waiting. The reasons for his waiting now become clear (vv. 22-24). The tone of these verses is one of trust. Covenant language rules (v. 22). Steadfast love or loving-kindness and mercy characterize the LORD's attitudes toward and commitment to covenant partners. Steadfast love is not primarily an emotional sentiment. Rather it implies fidelity to covenant obligations. It should be noted that it is the attitude of God, not the human covenant partner. The word for "mercy" is related to the Hebrew word for "womb." It suggests womb-love, the kind of passionate attachment that a mother has for the child of her womb. Again, this is a divine—not a human—characteristic. If the strong man can claim such a covenant relationship with God, he certainly has grounds for hope.

Once again the Hebrew is not clear (v. 22). The first-person plural form of the verb suggests that "we have not been cut off" because of the steadfast love of the LORD. If this reading is adopted, the strong man would here be identifying his suffering with that of all of the people and would be speaking in their name, declaring that their sufferings have not totally destroyed them. However, most translations consider steadfast love and mercy as the compound subject, and they emend the verb to read "they have not been cut off." With this reading the strong man would be proclaiming that neither steadfast love nor mercy has been terminated. Rather, like the light of day or the early dew, they are renewed each morning. The strong man speaks directly to God when he states that such steadfastness is evidence of God's faithfulness, yet another covenant characteristic. Thus, this battered man does indeed have reason for hope. It is rooted in the steadfast love, mercy, and faithfulness of God.

The expression of hope ends with a declaration: "The LORD is my portion" (v. 24). This metaphor calls to mind the apportionment of land to the tribes of Israel. Each one received a parcel of land, with the exception of the tribe of Levi, the tribe from which came the priests of Israel. Aaron, the representative of the priests, was told by God: "You shall have no inheritance in the land; I am your portion" (Num 18:20). They would not find security and peace in land or in the prosperity that might accrue from it. Instead, they were to depend on God who would take responsibility for their well-being. Having been stripped of both land and possessions, the strong man uses this metaphor to proclaim that God is all that he needs for survival, that God will provide for him just as God promised to provide for Aaron and his descendants. This declaration is not made superficially; it comes from the man's soul, his life force. The passage ends as it began: "Therefore will I hope [in him]."

Theological and Ethical Analysis

Trust in God in the midst of difficulties may seem to some to be the last resort. However, the hope that is proclaimed here (3:21-24) is not to be minimized or scorned. Nowhere does the strong man voice a desire for release from his tribulations or a return to better times. He does not hope *for* something; rather, he hopes *in* someone. He does not set any agenda for God; rather, he turns toward God alone and he waits. He calls on some of the most profound covenant features—steadfast love, mercy, and faithfulness—features that characterize God in a way that is diametrically opposed to the picture of God that he painted earlier (vv. 1-20). Any hope that this man might harbor is grounded in God's own fidelity to the covenant that God initiated, a covenant which human beings may spurn but which God always upholds. This is as disinterested a hope as might be found in the human heart. Though one trusts in God's promises, it is because one trusts in the God who makes the promises.

THE LORD IS GOOD: 3:25-39

Exegetical Analysis

Having proclaimed his own confidence in God's covenant characteristics, the strong man provides his audience with a series of statements that resemble didactive instruction. Though descriptive in form, each statement functions in a rhetorical fashion; each suggests a way of handling the misfortunes of life. The content addresses suffering generally. It does not seem to correspond with the torment that the strong man himself endured. In many ways individual verses and triads of verses appear to be independent of each other, merely included in order to comply to the acrostic structure. However, in several places the verses are connected with each other by means of catchwords or similar ideas.

Each of the first three lines (vv. 25-27) begins with the word "good." As has been the case in so many other places in the book, there is an irregular use of pronouns. Verse 25a uses the plural, while verse 25b has the singular. Verse 26a returns to the plural, and verse 27 has the singular again. Because of this irregularity, some commentators have emended the text in ways that seem to be unnecessary since such diversity of expression is common in poetry. First and foremost, it is the LORD who is good (v. 25). While this declaration may pertain particularly to the verse in which it is found, it also sets the context for the entire passage, thus indicating that God is good even in the face of what appears to be divine punishment.

The strong man begins his instruction by stating that those who wait for, depend upon, or trust in the LORD will experience divine goodness. Although the word for "trust" differs from the one found earlier (vv. 21, 24), it functions in a way similar to that of the catchword, connecting this verse with what precedes it. The strong man declares that he waits for or hopes in the LORD. He might well be including himself here in the company of those who will experience God's goodness because they seek God or have trusted in God. The word for "seek" implies an aggressive and persistent searching. The one who diligently seeks yet patiently waits for the LORD will surely enjoy God's goodness.

The earlier word for "wait" appears again ("wait quietly," v. 26), continuing the use of catchwords as well as the introductory word "good." It is not enough to wait for the LORD. This waiting should be done in silence and resignation, in anticipation of the salvation that God will grant. The Hebrew states that it is good that a strong man has to bear his yoke while he is a youth (v. 27). Did the speaker perhaps have himself in mind when he said this? The metaphor "yoke" is quite interesting. Yokes were placed upon the necks of beasts of burden in order to control them, to keep them on a straight course. A yoke is a sign of submission. Used metaphorically it also implies suffering. The verse suggests that it is good to be forced to endure misfortune when one is a youth, for during those formative years suffering can serve a disciplinary or even a redemptive function. The image of a strong man yoked in submission is an obvious contradiction. However, it underscores the comprehensive nature of the misfortune endured and it does correspond with the description of suffering found earlier in the poem (vv. 1-20). Although these verses follow immediately upon the expression of hope, they do not presume that suffering will be removed or withheld from those who trust in God. Rather, they indicate the good that can be derived from suffering if it is accepted and allowed to accomplish its educative and even salvific ends.

Instruction on how to deal with suffering continues. The next three verses (vv. 28-30) begin with verbs in a hortatory form: Let him sit; let him put his mouth; let him offer. Though hard to hear, the teaching insists that it is appropriate that the one suffering should sit alone and be silent when the yoke is placed upon him. The allusion to the yoke and the second reference to waiting quietly link this verse with verses 27 and 26 respectively. Rather than open his mouth in speech, the one suffering is admonished to put his mouth to the dust, a sign of complete self-abasement (v. 29; cf. v. 16). Hope, the desired goal of such self-abasement, is a catchword that links this verse with verse 25. The movement from sitting alone and in silence to humbling oneself in the dust is brought to conclusion with the acts of offering one's cheeks to someone who will smite them and of handing oneself over to mockery. This is a movement from simple suffering to self-imposed humiliation to shaming at the hands of another. In each case, the one who suffers the humiliation and shame does so willingly, a situation apparently quite different from that experienced by the strong man of the poem.

The list of reasons for placing one's trust in God continues to grow (vv. 31-33). The first verse of this triad (v. 31) maintains that the tribulation that one must endure will eventually come to an end, for God does not turn away forever from those who are oppressed. The second verse (v. 32) is even more reassuring for the sufferer. Using covenant language, it states that while God does cause affliction, motivated by steadfast love God will ultimately show mercy. As was stated earlier (v. 22), this covenant language points to God's fidelity to covenant commitment. The third verse (v. 33) suggests an explanation for God's fierce behavior. It claims that God is anything but capricious. In fact, God unwillingly causes suffering. Once again the covenant agreement is at work. It is human infidelity that compels God to chastise those who have disregarded their own covenant obligations. Here human beings are called "sons of adam." This gender-biased reference could be to Adam, the progenitor of the human race, or to the collective "humankind." In either case the phrase refers to people in general. These sentiments exonerate God, for while God is the cause of the suffering in the world, God is not really morally responsible for it—human sin is.

The next three verses (vv. 34-36) have challenged translators. Each verse begins with an infinitive. The only finite verb is found at the very end of the triad ("does the LORD not see it," v. 36*b*). Many commentators maintain that the entire unit depends upon this main verb. The awkwardness of such a structure has led others to argue that the sense here flows from the thought of the preceding verse (v. 33). The ills described here are social evils generated by the circumstances of tyrannical rule. While the incarceration of prisoners may be appropriate, the exploitation of their vulnerable situation is a miscarriage of justice; the violation of the fundamental God-given rights of anyone, friend or foe, innocent or guilty, is a deplorable act; and the subversion or undermining of the legal cause of another is reprehensible. Regardless of how one relates these statements with those that precede them or with those that follow, God does not seem to be held responsible for such heinous acts. Perhaps God does not see them, as some translations suggest. But if this is the case, how is one to understand the all encompassing wisdom of God, particularly when God is identified here as the Most High (v. 35)?

Through the use of rhetorical questions, the strong man concludes his instruction with a clear assertion of God's control over all human events (vv. 37-38). Only divine decrees are irrevocably fulfilled; only the Most High God can ordain both what is evil and what is good. This point of view is fundamental to the sapiential or wisdom tradition, particularly creation theology. It is there that we find the tenet that all things are under God's control, because God is the creator of all things. While it may be difficult to understand how a good God can be responsible for what appears to be evil, it is even more difficult for one who believes that there is only one God to conceive of anything, even what is evil, as having originated from outside of that one God.

The theological dilemma of innocent suffering is resolved in the final verse of this unit (v. 39). Here the strong man asserts that no living person really has the right to complain. After all, that person still has life, and with life there is always a chance that things will improve. The mercy of God may still be savored in the future (v. 22). Only the dead have no hope. Furthermore, a sinner, especially one who is in some kind of covenant relationship with God, is in no position to protest what is probably just desserts for infidelity. This last statement brings to conclusion the insistence that the suffering endured was retribution for sin. This resolution then absolves God of any culpability.

Theological and Ethical Analysis

Theological issues in this unit (3:25-39) are both similar to and different from those in the preceding one. The theme that most binds them together is that of hope. Despite the commonality, this theme unfolds in quite different ways in these two passages. Previously, the ground of hope was God's covenantal trustworthiness. Here, it is one of the attitudes that suffering people are encouraged to develop. The previous passage featured the steadfast love and mercy of God. Here, the justice of God is dominant. It is clear that the prevailing image of God and the character of one's relationship with that God shape the contours of one's hope.

The context for this reflection is human suffering. In the face of it, many people struggle to endure. In the face of it, their faith in God is often tested. Women and men frequently compound their agony when they fight suffering. Still, their human instinct for survival compels them to resist what they fear might destroy them, for in surrendering to it they might succumb to despair. The challenge is for the strong man or strong woman to stand bravely in the midst of overwhelming affliction. In times like this they may hope for a reprieve, or at least for some dimension of understanding. In times like this it is quite natural to wonder whether it is possible simply to trust that all things are in the hands of a wise and loving God, as the religious tradition maintains. From the point of view of the one suffering, such sentiments may appear to be beyond human possibility, perhaps even futile. Yet there are times when many individuals are actually catapulted into such radical heroism, when there is nowhere to turn except to God, when there is nothing else to do except to hope. The mystical traditions of theology claim that at such times many people simply reach deep within themselves in order to find there something that will enable them to endure. There they discover strength that they never imagined they possessed, a strength that could only come from God.

When people are able to do this, their afflictions can become the arena wherein they learn profound lessons about life, about human vulnerability and strength, about transcendence and transformation, and about God. When they can do this, even their questions seem to take on a different tone. They no longer ask how they will be able to endure, for they seem to have discovered ways to endure and to be transformed through the suffering. They no longer question why God has done this, for they seem to be more concerned with what God might be inviting them to become through their suffering. This way of dealing with misfortune may appear somewhat heroic, and yet it is probably more common than one might think. When people cannot avoid suffering, when they cannot understand it, many people plumb the depths of their spirits and try to carry on, living with dignity and grace.

Finally, there is much to be said about paying for one's mistakes and learning the hard lessons that this has to teach. It is not that the balance of the universe has been compromised and only punishment can correct the asymmetry, as some ancient societies may have thought. Rather, it seems that many limited, bumbling, selfish human beings are only willing to correct mistakes if some form of recompense is required of them. Ethical compulsions can sometimes succeed where covenant integrity has been compromised. Harsh recompense is meant to prevent a repeat of unacceptable behavior, and the seriousness of the offense should determine the degree of retribution exacted. All of this presumes, of course, what this particular passage from Lamentations implies—that the one suffering is guilty of moral misbehavior and that the suffering is just recompense for such misbehavior.

Let Us Return to the Lord: 3:40-47

Exegetical Analysis

Up to this point in the poem, the strong man has spoken in first person singular. Here (vv. 40-47) he becomes the spokesperson of the community, speaking in first-person plural, sometimes to the community itself, sometimes directly to God. Despite the significantly different point of view, this unit is thematically linked with the preceding one and it also contains several of the ideas of the earlier individual lament (vv. 1-20). The unit manifests various traits of the communal lament, namely, accusation against God, complaint about enemies, and explicit lament.

The strong man further develops the theme of human culpability (vv. 40-42), a theme that was stated in the preceding unit. Turning to his community, he exhorts his compatriots to examine their manner of living and to reform their lives (v. 40). "Return" or "turn back" became a technical term that implies remorse for transgressions and return to God in sincere repentance. This plea for reflection and repentance is an admission of guilt. In a second entreaty, he calls for the lifting up of hands, a common gesture of prayer. The Hebrew can yield either "lift your hearts to your hands" or "lift your hearts along with your hands." The first version implies that the people's heartfelt sentiments should not be hidden within themselves, but should be lifted up to God; the second indicates that their prayer should be more than mere external formality. In both versions, the basic sense of the verse is the same: Prayer should be sincere, originating from the heart.

The strong man's call to repentance turns into a prayer of confession (v. 42). Identifying his plight with that of the entire people, he speaks to God in their name, admitting his and their common unfaithfulness: "We have transgressed and rebelled." Both Hebrew words that denote their infidelity mean "rebellion." Theirs is no minor transgression; it is a serious breach of the nation's relationship with God. Only a wholehearted return to God would be able to effect reconciliation after such rebellion. However, even if they would decide to repent and return to God, reconciliation is not in their hands. In the face of their defiance, God has withheld the kind of forgiveness that only God can give.

A series of dynamic metaphors describes the ferocity of God's attitude toward the sinful people: "wrapped yourself in anger ... pursued ... killed" (vv. 43-45). There is some question about the form of the verb "to wrap" (v. 43). Some read it as a simple active verb, yielding "you have wrapped us." Others consider it a reflexive verb and, influenced by the sense of that same verb in the next verse, they render it "you have wrapped yourself." The second version is preferred here. As mentioned above, this communal lament includes several of the images contained in the individual lament found in the first part of the poem. The picture drawn of a God driven by anger is the first such similarity (v. 1). Wrapped in fury, God pursues and slays the people, showing no pity. Other similarities follow. Just as the strong man's earlier personal prayer was shut out from God (v. 8), here the people's prayer cannot pierce the impenetrable cloud that is wrapped around God. They have been shamed before all other nations, just as the strong man became a laughingstock before them (v. 14). They are like scum or offscouring, perhaps even bodily waste, and garbage. In this despicable state all of their enemies jeer at them (v. 46; cf. 2:16a). God has definitely not only turned away from them, but also turned against them.

The final verse of this unit (v. 47) characterizes the helplessness of the people. Two pairs of words demonstrate the poetic skill involved. "Panic" captures the sense of the people's extreme emotional state; "pitfall" describes a hole dug in the ground as a trap to catch them; "devastation" and "destruction" are synonyms that refer to their social and political collapse. In Hebrew, these two phrases (*pahad wāpahat* and *hass̆ ē't w^ehassā ber*) are examples of both alliteration, the repetition of the same consonantal sounds, and assonance, the repetition of the same vowel sounds. The repetition itself reinforces the ideas expressed.

Theological and Ethical Analysis

Three distinct yet related theological themes dominate this unit (3:40-47). They are: the people's heinous sin; divine fury in the face of betrayal; and the ridicule of the nation's enemies. The description of the sin of the people is a continuation of the theme with which the previous unit closed. It is only fitting that it should be the first one treated here, because it explains God's attitude toward the sinner. It may be true that, as stated earlier (v. 39), the wicked really have little grounds to complain about punishment for their sinfulness. Still, here, the strong man is advocating admission of guilt and a sincere turning to God in prayer. Whether or not God will hear their prayer is entirely out of their hands. Repentance and prayer can never be considered a bargaining chip with which one hopes to coerce God's hand. All one can do is wait for God to respond (cf. Pss 39:7; 130:5-6). What is important is that responsibility for one's actions is assumed and the consequences of these actions are accepted, regardless of how severe these consequences may be.

Depicting God in an anthropological fashion serves various ends. Chief among them is that it provides us with a means of conceiving of a personal relationship with God. From this flow descriptions of God's delight in, concern regarding, and passionate love for us as well as divine disappointment in, frustration with, and anger in the face of our infidelity. Our religious traditions tell us that the latter, rather negative attitudes really spring from the former, positive ones. From this point of view, one might say that the intensity of divine rage reflects both the degree of God's fundamental love for us and the seriousness of our disregard for this love. This is the picture of God sketched in these verses.

Finally, the derision that their enemies heap upon the beleaguered people demonstrates the depths to which human callousness can descend. The people's visible situation of misfortune, even more than their culpability, prompts others to berate them. Contempt adds insult to injury. Too often people choose to disassociate themselves from those in need rather than comfort them or provide them with assistance. Although it is possible to point to examples of great magnanimity in the face of the misfortune of others, there are times when human solidarity is one of the casualties of adversity.

I AM LOST; HEAR ME: 3:48-57

Exegetical Analysis

As abruptly as the strong man earlier shifted from first-person singular pronouns to the plural (vv. 40-47), so he returns to the use of the singular here. Some commentators maintain that, despite the singular forms used, verses 48-51 really belong to the previous communal lament, since here the strong man is still focusing on the sufferings of the broader population and not exclusively on his own. They argue that he is now functioning as the personification of the people, the "I" being a communal "I." This interpretation does not seem to be necessary or appropriate, since the city and the nation have been consistently personified as female, Daughter Zion (v. 2:1) and Daughter Judah respectively (v. 2:2). Despite the change in pronouns, it is clear that the strong man is once again describing his own tribulation.

The word "destruction" links this unit with the previous one (cf. v. 47). Destruction has so devastated the strong man that he is overcome with grief and his eyes stream with tears (vv. 48, 51). His tears are genuine, not like those of the professional mourners who are paid to manifest grief. He will have no respite from weeping until the LORD looks down from heaven and sees (vv. 49-50). In this context, heaven does not merely denote the place of divine dwelling. It also connotes the vast distance between God and the suffering people, designated here as "the daughter of my people" and "the daughters of my city." There is also an added connotation to the meaning of "see." It suggests that if God sees, God will do something about the situation that is seen (cf. 1:9c, 11c).

The strong man turns back to the consideration of his own plight. He uses three figurative expressions to characterize his misfortune (vv. 52-54). In an earlier lament (vv. 1-20), God was his attacker, the one who walled him in, who threatened his life. Here the enemies are human. First, he likens himself to a helpless bird for whom his enemies have set a snare. To underscore the tragedy of his predicament, he insists that there is no reason for their enmity. There is neither political, nor social, nor personal history that might explain their hostility. Second, he says that his captors have treated him like an apprehended animal. They have cut off his life by throwing him into a cistern, a pit into which they then threw stones in an attempt to put him to death. (There is a comparable incident in the life of the prophet Jeremiah in the book that bears his name [Jer 38:4-6]. This similarity is another reason why some maintain that either the narrator in this book or the strong man of this chapter is really Jeremiah.) Since the word for "stone" is singular, some believe that one stone was affixed to the opening of the pit, thus entombing the man. Finally, he cries out that he is in water up to his head. Since the other expressions were figures of speech, this one is also probably one as well. His circumstances overwhelm the strong man; he feels like he is drowning in them. In the face of all of this he cries out: "I am lost!"

Scholars dispute the interpretation of the verbs in the next section (vv. 55-57), because the tenses are not consistent. Some are perfect, indicating completed action (past tense in English usage), while others are imperfect denoting incomplete action (present tense). The issue at hand is whether the prayer to God and God's response to that prayer happened in the past or are happening in the present. If the verbs are meant to be present tense, the passage would be an example of dynamic faith and trust. On the other hand, a report of past divine pleasure could inspire hope that God will act in the present and the future with the same graciousness experienced earlier. Appeal to God and trust that God will respond are operative in either reading of the verbs.

Earlier the strong man reported that his enemies had thrown him into a pit (v. 53). Now he says that he cried out to God from the deepest recesses of that pit (cf. Ps 130:1-2). Some commentators maintain that this is a reference to the pit of death or the underworld. However, it is not necessary to understand the text in this way. In poetry such as this, which reflects on examples of extreme torment, it is quite common to characterize tribulation as an experience of death. Earlier the agonizing man pleaded that God would see his suffering. Now he begs God to hear his prayer. In both instances there is an implicit hope that God will be attentive to his needs. A very unusual word appears in verse 56b. It is a form of the word for breath, and it has been variously translated as "relief," "groaning," and "gasping." Any of these versions fits the man's cry: "Do not shut your ear to me!"

The statement in verse 57 contradicts that of verse 44. In the earlier verse, the strong man asserted that his prayer was unable to reach God. Here he claims that in the past God did indeed hear him, in fact, drew near to him and spoke to him in reassuring words: "Do not fear!" How is one to reconcile this apparent contradiction? Is the man recalling a much earlier experience of God, from a time when he enjoyed a favorable relationship with God? Does he call on the goodwill of that time in order to persuade God to act in a comparable compassionate manner? Probably so. In which case, he would be grounding his hope for the future in the experience of the past.

Theological and Ethical Analysis

Solidarity with victims and trust in God occupy our attention here (3:48-57). Women and men of integrity can be shaken to the depths of their beings when they witness other people having their loved ones snatched from their arms, being stripped of possessions, and publicly shamed. Everyone's human dignity is assaulted when lives are systematically dismantled, when human potential is nipped in the bud, when hopes and dreams are dashed against the rocks of cruelty. In Lamentations the strong man responded intensely to the tragedy that he witnessed, although one may wonder whether his response would have been as heartfelt had he not experienced that tragedy himself. Yet many people are not so moved. Elie Wiesel, himself a survivor of the Nazi holocaust, knew from experience that people can indeed stand by dispassionately and do nothing while others are hunted down, tortured, and put to death. Too many times a detached world has looked on passively as individuals, cities, or whole populations are destroyed. In such situations, it not only appears that God is locked away in the heavens, but that human beings have absolved themselves of any responsibility to step in and offer help. Our times have seen this happen again and again. These are issues of justice, and righteousness cries out for compassion.

One might ask on what grounds trust in God is based. Though this is definitely a theological question, the answer may sound somewhat anthropocentric: As with everything else in life, trust in God is probably based in experience. At the time of the exile, the people of ancient Israel trusted in God because their ancestors had earlier already experienced God's goodness ("in you they trusted, and were not put to shame" [Ps 22:5]). In addition to this religious perspective, the common inclination of trusting in someone or something beyond human reality suggests the fundamental hopeful character of the human spirit. Even those who have known only hardship and heartache look to the future for a change in fortune. This can be seen in Israel's prayer ("When I am afraid, I put my trust in you" [Ps 56:3]). When such optimism arises, the question is seldom: Why do we trust? It is instead: In whom, or in what do we trust?

PAY THEM BACK: 3:58-66

Exegetical Analysis

Cries of lament and expressions of hope conclude with a prayer for justice. A series of verbs lays the foundation for the strong man's plea to God: You have championed; you have redeemed; you have seen; you have heard (vv. 58-61). There is a distinct juridical character to the first two verses. "Cause" (v. 58) refers to disputation in court; "to judge" (v. 59) means to decide controversial civil, domestic, or religious cases; a second "cause" (v. 59) denotes the litigation brought before a civil magistrate. It is clear that the strong man's prayer is an appeal to divine justice. Verse 58 continues the declaration of God's previous attentiveness to the needs of the man which is found in verse 57. This declaration is so inconsistent with the relentless accusation against God that comprises the bulk of this poem. Now the man uses language that intimates a close relationship between himself and God. In many traditional societies as was ancient Israel, the legal responsibility "to redeem" (v. 58) rests on the shoulders of kinfolk. To announce that God has redeemed his life is to claim that God has acted toward him as would a member of his family (cf. Lev 25:35). The picture of God here is no longer one of an attacker, as has been the case throughout the man's complaints. Instead, God is blood kin, the one who will rescue him from his predicament.

The strong man declares that God has indeed seen how his enemies have wronged him, how he has been made the victim of the malice of others. God has heard their derision. Now, as in a court of justice, all of this incriminating evidence against them is placed before God. The strong man pleads for the divine judge to act in his defense. Although he has had to endure the plots that his enemies have devised against him, it is the way that they have shamed him that seems to have caused him the most distress. They taunt him and speak against him all day long (v. 62). The expression "sit and rise" (v. 63) forms a merism, an idiomatic expression consisting of two words that represent a totality. For example, mountains and valleys comprise the whole countryside; heaven and earth make up the universe. "Sit and rise" represents all of one's daily activities. Here it implies that regardless of the activity in which his enemies are engaged, he is the butt of their taunt songs. Once again we see that the loss of honor is the most keenly felt deprivation.

The strong man concludes his words on the harshest of notes, in a prayer of imprecation rife with the sting of vengeance: "Pay them back!" (v. 64). The man who has suffered so bitterly asks God to repay his assailants with the same brutality with which they have attacked him: Give them what they deserve! Although the Hebrew in verse 65 is quite obscure, its foreboding tone is unmistakable. This man does not merely ask God to punish his persecutors; he asks God to curse them. He further asks God to pursue these people with the same fiery wrath with which God previously pursued him, to apprehend them and destroy them. Unlike many individual laments, this prayer does not end with confidence in God's mercy. It ends on a note of vindictiveness: They too have sinned and so God should punish them as well.

Theological and Ethical Analysis

The sentiments with which the poem ends (3:58-66) are distressing indeed. Not only is there a lack of forgiveness on the part of the man, but he actually seeks to enlist God as an accomplice who will administer the vengeance with which his heart is filled. This is not only an unsavory picture of human revenge, but it portrays God as vicious and vindictive. Two important points should be discussed at this juncture. The first is the question of justice. To call upon God to redress an unjust situation can certainly be considered a religious act. It is true that the man admitted that he and his compatriots were guilty of sin and rebellion (v. 42) and, therefore, are deserving of some form of punishment. However, earlier in this poem, he spoke of the covenant attitudes of steadfast love and mercy (v. 22), implying that there is an intimate relationship between himself and God. From this perspective, he might well have believed that any attack on a covenant partner of God is an attack on God, an attack that deserves swift and burning reprisal.

The second point has to do with the agent of revenge. The man does not appoint himself the arbiter of justice. He does not take matters into his own hands and retaliate after the example of Lamech, who justified a seventy times sevenfold vengeance against those who had offended him (Gen 4:24). Instead, this man entrusts the situation to the judgment of God. He asks that his enemies be punished by God according to their deeds.

Questions of justice and divine agency notwithstanding, the hatred which the man harbors is fierce, and he entreats God to enter into it with him. Having admitted that he and the rest of his people have rebelled against God, he does not entertain the possibility that his enemies are simply the means through which God has decided to punish him and his people for their sins. True, they may have been God's special covenanted people, but that only makes their infidelity all the more grievous. They were in a special relationship with God, and disloyalty to that relationship was a form of treachery. Finally, as tragic as this man's plight may be, he does not seem to be motivated by religious zeal. He is not merely seeking justice; he wants vengeance. He does not simply ask that God punish the others; he wants God to curse them, to destroy them. While such sentiments may erupt quite naturally in the heart of one who has experienced what this strong man describes has been his lot, it is very difficult—though not impossible—to attribute unambiguous religious motivation to his petition. It is on this savage and vengeful note that the poem ends.

COMMENTARY

LAMENTATIONS 4

SOCIETY HAS COLLAPSED

Literary Analysis

A noticeable shift in both structure and content takes place in this chapter. Although this poem conforms to an acrostic pattern, as did the previous ones, it contains two lines of poetry for each letter of the alphabet, rather than three lines as found in each of the first three chapters of the book. This shortening of length suggests that the book itself follows a 3 + 2 *qinah* structure (see Introduction) associated with the funeral dirge. There is also a decided change in the character of the description contained in this chapter. The speaker is presumably the same narrator as was found in chapters 1 and 2. However, his manner of reporting the disaster seems to be subdued here in contrast to the earlier accounts. While some commentators see this as the narrator's emotional distancing, it can also be interpreted as a literary device used by the poet to reinforce the dirgelike character of the entire book. In other words, the first three chapters overflow with strong emotion and, by comparison, the emotion in this chapter (as well as that in the one that follows) is somewhat restrained. Just as the three line pattern of the first three chapters is followed by shortened lines in the last two chapters suggesting a *qinah*-like structure (3+2), so the strong emotional expression of those three chapters is followed by a lessening of emotional response in the last two. Thus, in both structure and emotional tenor, this book resembles the 3+2 character of the mournful *qinah*.

The chapter contains features of both the dirge and the lament, making an exact identification of genre quite difficult. For the sake of the present examination, the content is divided into three parts:

1-16   a dirgelike description of the suffering endured by various groups within the beleaguered city;
17-20   a communal lament;
21-22   a taunt song.

Finally, verse 15 is longer than the rest of the verses in the poem. In order to remedy this and thereby produce a verse that conforms to the metric pattern of the poem, some commentators shorten it. This is not necessary for, though it is different, the line is in an acceptable *qinah* meter.

After the Fall: 4:1-16

Exegetical Analysis

Following the pattern set by the previous chapters, this poem opens with the dirgelike exclamation "Ah!" or "Ah how!" *('êkāh)*. Once again the narrator chokes back a cry of indescribable distress. A second feature of the dirge follows, namely, the recounting of the reversals of fortune. Like some of the reversals found in earlier poems (1:1-11), these reversals report the plight of specific groups of inhabitants: the children (vv. 1-4); the well-to-do (v. 5); the inhabitants in general (v. 9). Also in keeping with the character of the dirge, the reversals report the deaths of these people. To accomplish this, various metaphors are employed, all pointing to the famine that withered not only the bodies of the populace but also their spirits.

Although the Hebrew of the first line of verse 1 is uncertain, most commentators maintain that the reference is to the changing or tarnishing of gold. A problem in interpretation arises because gold does not really tarnish as does silver. However, this fact only serves to emphasize the magnitude of the reversal which the poet reported. While people value gold as one of the most precious metals on earth, tarnished gold is worthless. If it did tarnish, it would lose its value and would most likely be discarded. The meaning of the second metaphor is also somewhat ambiguous. The stones are called "holy." Though most commentators argue against interpreting them as either the stones from the destroyed temple or the gems from the vestments of the high priest, to call them "holy" is to suggest that they are in some way sacred. Once again, the words chosen emphasize the magnitude of the reversal. What were once revered as consecrated or holy are scattered at the corner of every street.

Of what is the narrator speaking? What is without value, like tarnished gold? What is scattered, like discarded stones? The referent of these two metaphors is found in verse 2; it is the children of Zion. Although the Hebrew has "sons," it is clear from the context that the narrator means both sons and daughters. By means of yet a third metaphor (clay pot), the narrator describes a final reversal. The potter's hand may indeed produce a work of art, but it would be a lackluster artifact made from the clay of the earth and, because of the frailty of its composition, this pottery can easily break. In no way can an earthen pot compare in brilliance, value, or endurance with gold or precious stones. These three metaphors depict Zion's precious children, once "worth their weight in gold," not debased, presumably broken and, therefore, discarded as if worthless.

The narrator characterizes the plight of the children by comparing the behavior of the citizens of the city with that of two animals that are normally disdained by human beings (v. 3): the jackal and the ostrich. The jackal is a wild doglike animal about the size of a fox. A scavenger and carrion eater that roams deserted places, it is the kind of animal that would be found to frequent a ruined city like Zion. As despicable as such an animal might seem to humans, it does care for its young. Acting out of its nurturing instinct, the female offers her breast so that her young might suckle. In contrast, the people of Zion are compared to the ostrich that appears to be unconcerned with the fate of its young. The female lays eggs in the sand and then leaves them unprotected to hatch by themselves in the sun (cf. Job 39:13-16).

The Hebrew in this verse (v. 3b) is literally translated as "my daughter," leading many to conclude that the narrator is condemning the behavior of mothers. However, there are at least two reasons that suggest that the reference is more likely to the population in general. First, the same phrase appeared in an earlier poem (2:11). Since the reference there was to the entire people, the phrase probably carries the same meaning throughout this poem (vv. 3, 6, 10). Second, since the comparison is to the action of the female jackal and ostrich, though the male ostrich seems to show no more interest in the young than does his mate, the word "daughter" seems appropriate. In other words, the narrator is condemning not only the callousness of the mothers, but that of the entire adult population, a population with which the narrator himself identifies ("my people"). The people have not taken the necessary precautions that would safeguard the welfare of the children. As a result, the vulnerable children suffer the ravages of hunger and thirst.

The parched tongue of the suckling child cleaves to the roof of its mouth (v. 4a). This might be the result of the neglect described above or of the famine described in the following verses. Those commentators who place all of the blame on the heartless mothers suggest that, unlike the mother jackals, the human mothers refuse to offer their breasts to the nurslings. However, starving women do not have milk to offer their children. Whichever way these verses are understood, it is clear that the narrator is probably less concerned with those who are to blame for the plight of these infants than for the agony that the little ones endure. Besides the totally dependent nurslings, there are other children who struggle for survival (v. 4b). Young children beg for bread, but no one gives them anything to eat. As is so often the case in desperate straits such as the people seem to have encountered, the most vulnerable endure the greatest suffering. This is not only because of their extreme need, but also because they seldom possess the ingenuity required for discovering ways to survive.

The children were not the only victims of starvation; others faced the same fate. The wealthy who previously feasted on delicacies or rich food are now wasting away in the streets (v. 5a). The implication of this reversal of fortune is twofold. They are not only emaciated from lack of nourishment, but they are also out in the streets foraging for whatever food they might be able to find. Desperate need is here compounded by bitter shame. Their reversal of fortune is depicted in yet another way (v. 5b). Purple clothing, though traditionally associated with royalty, was also worn by the very wealthy. To be brought up in purple means to be raised in circumstances of privilege. Now the circumstances of those privileged are overturned and they sit on an ash heap. This site is probably not just a garbage dump. The description suggests that the refuse has been burned and only ashes remain. Those who formerly enjoyed being the elite of the population have now taken their place in the midst of destruction and disgrace.

Almost as an aside, the narrator moves from a description of the tribulations suffered by some of the inhabitants to a theological assessment of the plight of the entire population (v. 6) referred to again as "daughter of my people." The affliction endured is said to be greater than the punishment of Sodom, the city upon which fire fell from heaven (see Gen 19:24-25). This is an extraordinary assessment, for the sinfulness of Sodom was legendary (cf. Jer 23:14; Ezek 16:46-52), and to accuse another city of exceeding that level of iniquity was to plunge it into the depths of culpability. The affliction that flowed from the sinfulness of these two cities is contrasted in yet another way. As guilty as Sodom may have been, its tribulations fell upon it in an instant. Its destruction was immediate, not protracted as was the suffering of this reprobate city. Although the poem does not enumerate any of Zion's failings, earlier poems spoke of infidelity to covenant responsibilities (3:22-24), offenses that far exceed the reprehensible behavior of Sodom.

The Hebrew in the second part of verse 6b is uncertain. Some translate it to mean that no (human) hand was involved in executing Sodom's punishment, it being clearly the work of God. Others maintain that it suggests that no hand was turned to help that city. Still others hold that there were no wringing hands expressing anxiety or sorrow over the city's plight. Even in the face of this ambiguity, there is a common thread in all of the versions: At its darkest moment, Sodom received no human mediation. If Sodom was left alone in her misery, then how can Zion, whose sin and punishment far outstrip that of the doomed city, expect any kind of relief at the hands of human beings?

As the narrator continues his account of the affliction suffered by inhabitants of Zion, his attention turns to the royal leaders (vv. 7-8). Their privileged lives provided them with opportunities to pamper their bodies, thus ensuring that they would meet the standards of beauty in vogue at the time. Figures of speech characterize their former beauty. These favored ones are said to have been purer than snow and whiter than milk. Because the Hebrew that follows is unclear (v. 7b), scholars have advanced various translations of the verse. The most common version declares that their bones, a reference to their entire bodies, were the ruddy color of coral, and their "cut" was deep blue like precious sapphire. Several carvings showing tightly braided dark blue hair have survived from this period in history. These artifacts suggest that "cut" might be a reference to hair style. Despite these problems of translation, it is clear that the verse is meant to offer a contrast between the present situation of hardship and the indulgence of the past. Before the collapse of the city, royal leaders were striking in appearance. Now this is all changed and the reverse is true. Their once pure white countenance has become blacker than soot, due either to the fire that consumed so much of the city or to their macabre, desperate physical circumstances. Skin that was formerly healthy and robust is now shriveled and dry, the results of starvation and dehydration. Their deterioration is so drastic that when they are in public, people no longer recognize them. The reversal of fortune has been dramatic.

Many commentators maintain that the final mention of hunger (v. 9) is a reference to the conditions of these previously privileged rulers. However, it is a very general statement and, therefore, it could be simply a summary of the tribulations of the entire population. It states that it is better to die a swift even violent death at the point of a sword than to succumb to the slow, excruciating death of starvation. Life may be spilled in the first instance, but it drains agonizingly out of the body in the second. This second death is the one suffered by the nurslings and the young children (v. 4), by the well-to-do (v. 5), and by the inhabitants in general.

Starvation brought the people to the brink of the unspeakable, and their despair pushed them over the edge. They were reduced to cannibalism, one of the curses provoked by violation of covenant precepts (cf. Deut 28:53-57). If cannibalism was not horrendous enough, the narrator reports an example of the worst form of this barbarous practice—mothers boiled and ate the bodies of their own children (v. 10; cf. 2:20). The word "compassionate," which is used to describe these mothers, is related to the Hebrew word for womb. Thus, compassion came to be regarded as a form of womb-love. Use of the word underscores the heartrending horror of the situation at hand. The very ones who engendered womb-love boiled and ate the fruit of their wombs. There is no way of mitigating our abhorrence conjured up by such a scene. Having collapsed from the assault launched by outside enemies, the community ("daughter of my people") now suffers from its own inner disintegration.

In the character of a dirge, the narrator states that the tribulations endured by the city are the work of the LORD (v. 11). Three different words for fire describe divine anger. This assemblage of words underscores what is actually stated in the verse, namely, that the afflictions that have overwhelmed the people spring from the full force of God's wrath. It is almost as if disaster upon disaster has been thrown into a caldron, and their fury is just waiting to burst forth. When the boiling point is reached, they overflow with destructive power. This raging fury consumed Zion to her very foundations. Although the hungry tongues of fire most certainly devoured many of the city's structures, the language here is meant to be read metaphorically. It is the fire of God that destroys the city, not simply one set by her enemies. Supporting this interpretation is the fact that ancient cities generally were built on stone foundations, and this stone would probably not burn. In such circumstances, fire would consume whatever was built upon the foundations. By means of this metaphor, the narrator is claiming that the wrath of God has completely destroyed the city. There is nowhere that she can escape, there is nothing upon which she can depend.

Until the disastrous events actually occurred, the population of this once great city could not have even conceived of the possibility of its defeat (v. 13). Like most ancient cities, Zion was strategically built on a hill, giving it a commanding view of the surrounding plain below. However, the ultimate assurance of its inviolability rested neither in the advantage of its location nor in the extent of its military fortifications. Zion was considered impregnable because of the presence of God in its midst (cf. Pss 46:5; 48:1-3). The people were so confident of this that any statement that even suggested that the city might fall warranted the penalty of death (cf. Jer 26:11). To insist that the rulers of other nations were astounded at its defeat is probably exaggeration. However, the people themselves were grounded in Zion theology and, for that reason, such exalted language would be quite understandable.

The reason given by the narrator for the breach of Zion's gates by her enemies should be noted. He maintains that the prophets and the priests are responsible for the wrath of God that was unleashed on the city (vv. 13-16). Blaming the religious leaders for the afflictions that befell the city points to the religious dimension of the crimes that provoked such uncompromising punishment (2:14). The prophets were responsible for calling the people to covenant fidelity. Dereliction of this responsibility resulted in the people's faithlessness. The same was true with regard to the priests. They officiated over the religious rituals of the nation. They were the guardians of the practices of purity. Without them and their guidance the people would be denied ritual sacrifices and lacking in direction in matters of purity. Not only were these religious leaders derelict in their duties, which resulted in the sinfulness of others, but they were also guilty of shedding innocent blood.

There are many difficulties in the translation and interpretation of verses 14 and 15. It is not clear whether the blood that defiled the priests (v. 14) was the blood of the righteous alone (v. 13) or the blood of the wounded and dead in general. In any case, contact with blood made these religious leaders unclean and, therefore, unfit to act in any cultic capacity. Purity was a religious condition, not a moral one. It meant that one had met all of the conditions required for participation in cultic activity. These conditions included: respect for blood, the carrier of life; adherence to the orders of creation by eating only those foods judged "clean"; association only with those people who themselves observed the practices of ritual purity. Contact with certain bodily fluids, especially blood, rendered one unclean. This explains the taboos surrounding menstrual blood as well as birth blood, or bleeding at the time of death. The impurity of these prophets and priests was doubly heinous, for it was innocent blood that was shed, and they were the ones who shed it.

Ritual defilement was an appalling condition for any observant Israelite to endure, but it must have been particularly shameful for the priests (cf. Lev 21:11). However, being guilty of crime, these priests were now forced to endure its consequences. Not only were they defiled, but their defilement was made public, for their clothes were soaked in blood for all to see. Since people believed that ritual defilement was contagious, everyone avoided them. In fact, they were treated like lepers. The people shouted at them: "Unclean!" This was the word that lepers themselves were required to shout, warning the populace of the impending danger that contact with them might beget (v. 15; cf. Lev 13:45). The prophets and priests, the very ones to whom the lepers had to report their cure in order to be reinstated in the worshiping community, were themselves now treated like lepers. Recognizing the contamination that the religious leaders carry, the people rebuked them: "Do not touch!" and they cried out further: "Away!" With this latter command the religious leaders were expelled from the community and sentenced to lives of wandering, for not even the other nations were willing to take them in. There is a biting reversal here. The ones who were formerly held in the highest esteem are now publicly shamed, rebuked, and rejected.

The unit ends with yet another theological interpretation of the action of the LORD (v. 16). The Hebrew has "the face of the LORD," a phrase that is interpreted in various ways. Because the disposition of one's face reveals the focus of one's attention, the phrase can mean the "presence of the LORD." When it means "God's good pleasure," there is a presumption that God is looking kindly upon someone or something. Here God's face has turned away from the prophets and priests, meaning that God is hostile toward them, perhaps has even rejected them. Normally when God looks upon someone it is with eyes of love and concern. Although God might have looked upon the religious leaders in this way in the past, the provident face of God is turned toward them no longer. The narrator ends this dirgelike account with a second report of the loss of respect suffered by the priests. They are shown neither honor nor favor.

Theological and Ethical Analysis

In every national catastrophe, such as the one described here (4:1-6), those who are innocent of wrongdoing suffer alongside those who have lived lives of iniquity. If we believe that there is a direct correlation between morality and happiness or evil and tribulation, we may be little troubled over the afflictions rained on the wicked, but profoundly distraught over the plight of the innocent. Many will question why God has allowed these innocent to suffer. Others will question why, but will turn that question around and wonder why society has allowed the misfortune to happen, or what society might have done to prevent it. If the disaster is one of nature, the cause of the misfortune might be difficult to ascertain. However, if the adversity is in any way the result of societal circumstances, then a cause will be sought and the perpetrators pursued. Justice demands it; social harmony cannot exist without it.

There are many other believing people who do not subscribe to the idea of a strict retributive correlation. They do not believe that disastrous circumstances are always the consequences of human behavior. They do not agree with those who easily distinguish between the innocent and the guilty, considering as innocent all but the actual perpetrators of the tragedy. However, these people are no less bereaved by adversity of any kind and they too struggle to understand its cause. When they say that all things are in God's hands, they are not so much attributing the specifics of the catastrophe to God as they are voicing confidence in God's care even in the face of the disaster. Rather than believe that God afflicts human beings, they maintain that God cares for those who are afflicted.

Regardless of the circumstances or the cause of national calamity, most people consider the greatest tragedy to be the suffering of the children, especially the youngest and the most vulnerable. It has been said that the character of a people can be seen in the way they care for their children. This concern is not only because children are so helpless, but also because the future of the people rests in them. In this poem, the plight of the children is horrendous. It is bad enough that they wither away due to starvation and thirst. When they finally die, their lifeless bodies are further violated. They are boiled by their own mothers and their flesh is then consumed. Some commentators try to mitigate this horror by suggesting that the mothers act in such an appalling manner in their attempt to save the lives of other children who are starving but not yet dead. However, the text does not say that there are other children to save. It simply states that "they became their food." This shocking scene demonstrates the utter horror of the situation and the depths of degradation to which people have been reduced.

This passage also highlights the sinfulness of religious leadership. In the society depicted in the poem, such leaders wielded political as well as religious power. Therefore, it is correct to say that the passage highlights the failure of leaders in general. Time and again people engage in debates concerning the moral status of their leaders. Many believe that leaders should be held to a higher standard than the rest of society, because they are public people and the citizenry considers them models to emulate. Regardless of how one views this matter, there is no doubt about the influence that leaders exercise. They make decisions for and in the name of the group. They sometimes direct religious practices, and even shape religious thinking. They enact the laws by which people live, and they commit the citizenry to war or to peace with others. In many ways, leaders are certainly more responsible for the social, political, and religious state of the people than are most other citizens. Hence, their moral failure has a widespread effect on the nation.

Dashed Hopes: 4:17-20

Exegetical Analysis

An abrupt shift now takes place. The somewhat detached style of a third person reporting is replaced by an involved first person eyewitness account. Most commentators maintain that the narrator here identifies with the people of the doomed city and describes a portion of what the entire populace was forced to endure. The people looked for help from some other city, but their searching was in vain (v. 17). Those who believe that the poems of this book depict the destruction heaped upon Jerusalem by the Babylonians believe that the reference here is to Egypt. Mention of Edom in the following verses (vv. 21-22) has led others to consider that nation as the one that dashed the people's hopes. In either case, the verse is less concerned with the identity of the negligent nation than with the fact that it failed to come to the despairing city's assistance.

The people are forced to face their straits with no assistance from anyone. Their enemies dog their steps the way a hungry animal tracks its prey (v. 18); they lie in wait, ready to pounce on the unsuspecting. As a consequence, the people are prevented from walking through the streets, looking either to have their needs met or for an opportunity to flee. They are confined, and they realize that their days are numbered, their end is in sight. Escape is improbable, because those who pursue them are too swift for them to elude their grasp (v. 19). These pursuers are likened to the eagle. The tenor of this metaphor is multilayered. The eagle is noted for its remarkable speed. It is also a bird of prey. Related to the vulture, which feeds on carcasses, the eagle trains its keen eye on live quarry. The metaphor tells us that when the people attempted to escape, they were hunted down wherever they went by an enemy that possessed great precision. They were no safer in the confines of the mountains than they were in the open wilderness.

The king himself was involved in a thwarted attempt at escape (v. 20). Although he is not explicitly named, Zedekiah, the king who reigned during the time of Babylon's attack on Zion, made just such an attempt, but the Babylonians captured him (cf. 2 Kgs 25:1-7). Here the unnamed king bears two glorious titles: the breath of our life (literally, "breath of our nostrils"), and the anointed of the LORD. The second title is quite common and is one of the customary ways of characterizing the Israelite king. Although priests were also anointed with oil, thus setting them apart as sacred functionaries within the community, only the kings bore this title. Although the people of the realm enjoyed the blessings of the covenant that God entered into with the kings (see 2 Sam 7:8-16), only the kings were actual partners in that covenant. The first title, "breath of our life," is unusual in the tradition of Israel, but is a common title for Egyptian pharaohs. It implies that the life of the people is dependent upon the king. Together these two titles characterize the king as enjoying, on the one hand, a unique relationship with God and, on the other, an intimate relationship with the people.

The verses in this short passage begin and end with the realization of dashed hopes. Initial hope of being rescued by another nation was eventually seen to be futile (v. 17). Any hope that the people may have placed in the king, their divinely appointed leader, also proved to be ill-founded (v. 20). Formerly they had looked to him for protection; they thought that they were safe in his shadow. Now enemies have ravaged the city and its inhabitants, and the king has fled, only to be caught in the trap of his pursuers. It seems that all hope is lost.

Theological and Ethical Analysis

This passage (4:17-20) raises once again the question of trust. The inhabitants of this stricken city looked to their leaders for protection and to others for help. They turned for help to human ingenuity and military might. Faced with the incomprehensible, their hope seems to have been a kind of reactionary sentiment, appearing only when they themselves were unable to accomplish their goals unassisted.

The history of religious societies reveals that from earliest times women and men have been exhorted to trust in God alone; to hand themselves over unconditionally into the care of the divine; to do so hoping for nothing more than the courage and strength to hand themselves over unconditionally. These same religious traditions acknowledge that the very fundamental human vulnerability that prompts people to trust in the first place often prevents them from trusting completely. People need assurances, and since hope requires trust with no assurances, trust is very difficult to acquire. For this reason, they often settle for something less. Only the most courageous seem able to allow themselves to be vulnerable. Until people have reached this level of trust, most turn to fallible, ephemeral realities upon which to anchor themselves. Experience shows that hope grounded in such realities will eventually be dashed.

TAUNT AGAINST A NEIGHBOR: 4:21-22

Exegetical Analysis

The final verses of this chapter consist of a taunt hurled against Edom, a nation that bordered Israel (v. 21), and a message of hope for Zion (v. 22). Located on the eastern side of the Jordan River and southwest of Israel, Edom was a nation whose origin was traced back to Esau, the twin brother of Jacob. This meant that Israel and Edom came from the same ancestral family. One might expect that they would be allied and would feel some responsibility for each other. Such does not seem to have been the case. This text gives no hint of the reason for the rift between the two nations. Elsewhere we read that Edom did not come to the aid of Israel when, in its darkest hour, it suffered the horrors of invasion (cf. Obad 11; Ps 137:7). Here, with a kind of prophetic insight, the narrator announces that each of these nations will experience a significant reversal of fortune. Edom will be beset with affliction, while the torments that have plagued Zion will come to an end.

There is irony in the narrator's taunt: Rejoice and be glad, for you will be forced to endure unimagined suffering. The "cup of wine" is a very rich multilayered metaphor. It symbolizes the wrath of God (cf. Jer 25:15-29). A similar vessel was used in certain cursing ceremonies. It was filled with wine which represented the sufferings to be endured. This wine was then poured out, thus dramatizing the curse that was being poured out upon the people. Wine intoxicates and causes one to act in an uncharacteristic and sometimes unbecoming manner. So Daughter Edom is intoxicated with this wrathful wine, and she shames herself by exposing her nakedness.

Daughter Zion, on the other hand, has already borne tribulation upon tribulation. All of this has now come to an end. The text does not say that she is healed or that her prosperity is restored. It merely states that the punishment for her iniquity is over (v. 22). This verse contains one of the only explicit rays of hope contained within the book (3:22-24). It proclaims that Zion's cup of suffering is now filled to the brim; it is completed, finished. Her exile will be no more. This is promised. It is now Edom's turn to bear the chastisement that she has merited. In the previous verse Edom bared herself; here it is God who uncovers her sins, her nakedness, her shame. God metes out justice not only to Zion/Israel, but to Edom as well. These verses suggest that the justice of God covers all peoples. Earlier poems ended with prayers that beseeched God to afflict those who had caused Zion to suffer (cf. 1:22; 3:64-66). This poem clearly announces the misfortune that is in store for Edom. It is not expressed as a wish; it states with assurance what will take place in the future.

Theological and Ethical Analysis

Two themes stand out clearly in this short passage (4:21-22). The first is hope. Frequently the burden of suffering is eased when people can see light at the end of the tunnel. It means that they have endured and that the time of tribulation will soon be over. In their darkest moments, even the assurance that the end will indeed come can enliven their spirits and alleviate the weight that bears down upon them. The human spirit clings to even the slightest shreds of such hope. So often in the midst of tragedy people tell themselves, or they tell others: Everything is going to be all right. Whether this is true or false hope, they certainly want everything to be all right. They may even need such a flicker of hope in order to prepare themselves for a bleak future. Such proclamations of hope shows how desperately human beings need to hope in someone or something.

The second theme has to do with the attitude of women and men toward those who have wronged them. While a fervent desire that justice be meted out to them is certainly acceptable, there is a very thin line between such justice and wrathful vengeance. This is particularly true in a situation such as is depicted in the poems of this book. A city has been attacked; its people have been killed and its buildings destroyed. The loss of innocent life is obscene and the extent of devastation incalculable. It is appropriate that women and men of integrity stand up in righteous indignation. However, when they cry out angrily is it for justice or for blood? And in the heat of such anger, is it possible to make such a distinction? If it is genuine justice that they desire, how is it to be executed? It is impossible to relegate the exercise of justice to God alone, for societies cannot survive without the stability and social harmony that justice promises. There is no easy answer to this complex ethical predicament.

COMMENTARY

LAMENTATIONS 5

THE FINAL PETITION

Literary Analysis

The poem found in this chapter contributes to the overall *qinah* (3+2) structure of the entire book. This is a very short poem. Each verse contains only one line, unlike the three-line pattern found in the first three chapters and the two-line pattern of the fourth chapter. These features contribute to the sense of decreasing momentum, a characteristic of the *qinah*. In addition to this, it contains several unique literary characteristics in its own right. While it shares the twenty-two verse structure so common to the other poems, it is not actually an acrostic. The first words of each verse do not follow the order of the alphabet. Moreover, since the poem is not constrained by the alphabetic demands of an acrostic, it can more closely follow the format of a communal lament:

1	introductory petition
2-18	complaint to God
19	acknowledgment of divine sovereignty
20-22	final petition

The individual lines in this poem do not conform to the 3+2 *qinah* meter. Rather, they contain recognizable parallelism, a prominent feature of Hebrew poetry that highlights the correspondence of one reality with another. This correspondence can be one of equivalence or of contrast. The former kind of parallelism predominates here. A very graphic description serves as an example:

Women	are raped	on Zion,
virgins		in the towns of Judah (v. 11)

This poetic technique reinforces the ideas that are articulated in each verse. Finally, although this poem is significantly different from the other poems of the book, these features point to its remarkable poetic character.

REMEMBER, O LORD: 5:1-18

Exegetical Analysis

It is only in this chapter that the poem opens with an address directed to God: "Remember! . . . Look and see!" (v. 1). While it is not a usual characteristic of a dirge, petition is certainly a prominent feature of a lament such as this. Both lines in this parallel construction begin with imperative verbs. In Hebrew, the verb "remember" carries very rich meaning. It denotes not only an inner mental act, but, by implication, an appropriate external action. One remembers or calls to mind in order to do something about what is remembered. To ask God to remember a distressful situation is to ask God to remedy it. Since one of the major functions of parallelism is the correspondence between two lines, one can say that within the construction itself, the parallel elements interpret each other. Therefore, in this verse, "Remember" and "Look and see" mean basically the same thing.

The previous poems recounted many of the afflictions that befell the tormented inhabitants. However, the parallel construction suggests that here the lament focuses on the disgrace that the people endured. A people who took great pride in their election as the special people of God have been made to bear the humiliation of defeat. Those who depended upon God's presence in their midst to protect them from danger now feel abandoned by God and vulnerable in the presence of others. Their disgrace, which may have been the hardest blow to sustain, is twofold: their God seems either to have deserted them or to have been incapable of defending them; and their own strength did not match the overwhelming power of those who defeated them. Now they cry out to God: Attend to our plight, and do something about it.

The introductory cry to God is followed by a listing of some of the tribulations suffered by the people after their enemies conquered them and occupied their land (vv. 2-18). The first of these ordeals is the occupation itself. The land that once had been theirs, the land God had promised to them (see Gen 15:18) and which they considered their inheritance from God (see Deut 4:21), is now no longer under their control. It has been handed over to strangers, to aliens (v. 2). The verb is passive in form, implying that the occupiers were given the land by someone else. Was it God who did this? Did the God who first entrusted the people with the land now take it from them, only to give it to another nation? Although the text does not explicitly state this, it certainly does imply it.

In a patriarchal society political and social rights and responsibilities rest primarily on the shoulders of adult men. Widows and orphans are particularly vulnerable, because they have no male relative to attend to their societal needs. The people of this besieged city are described as orphans, and their mothers are like widows (v. 3). It is certainly possible that the men of the city were actually either killed or deported to another land. However, these characterizations can also be read figuratively. In other words, the entire population is now as defenseless as are widows and orphans. This certainly would be the situation if the city was under the control of an occupying force. Even if adult men had survived the attack, they would have no power of leadership, a circumstance that would contribute to their disgrace.

Having lost control of their homeland the people no longer manage the resources of that land, the water of streams and rivers and the wood of forests, the very staples of life. In order to survive, the disinherited inhabitants are now forced to purchase both the water that is essential for survival and that was once theirs for the taking, and the wood that will warm them and provide them with some kind of shelter (v. 4). Once again we see that insult is added to injury.

The Hebrew in verse 5 is very difficult to understand. Literally it reads: "Above our necks we are pursued." Some commentators translate the first part of the text to read "yoke," thus yielding: "With the yoke we are pursued." Because such a rendering seems awkward, they further emend the text to read: "With the yoke on our necks we are hard driven." A quite different reading is also possible. "Above our necks" means that something is beyond them; they have been overwhelmed by something. And what might this be? The text suggests that the people have been overwhelmed by the pursuit of others. The second line of the verse ("We are weary; we are given no rest") confirms either one of these readings. Both servitude to others, symbolized by the yoke, and pursuit by others would certainly be immensely difficult and wearisome.

The people are in such desperate straits that they are forced to turn to their mortal enemies for help (v. 6). The Hebrew phrase "given the hand to" has been understood in various ways. Some commentators argue that it is a reference to past alliances made with Egypt and Assyria. They maintain that it was just such alliances with foreign nations, alliances that demonstrated Israel's turn away from God's protection and to the security of human power, that resulted in God's retributive action. These commentators link the verse with the admission of past offenses found in the following verse (v. 7). Others interpret it as an agreement made for the sake of procuring food after the city was devastated. While it is true that at various times in its history, Israel counted both Egypt and Assyria as enemies, here they may represent the extent to which the people have had to humble themselves. This second reading keeps the focus of the complaint on the present difficulties endured by the populace. It corresponds with the theme of an earlier verse (v. 4), which states that the people had to buy water and wood from their occupiers.

The poet clearly states the guilt of ancestors (v. 7). However, these sinful ancestors are dead and the descendants are now forced to bear the guilt of their iniquity. With this statement, the people are not claiming their innocence. In a later verse (v. 16) the lament explicitly declares their culpability. Here they are merely acknowledging that as a people they have a history of disloyalty to God. It seems that God has unleased on this generation the fury of retribution.

The description of the humiliation borne by the defeated people continues. As if it were not bad enough that they are occupied by another nation, they are now ruled by servants of their occupiers (v. 8). These servants are probably minor officials, civil servants who played insignificant roles in their own country, but who now have been given jurisdiction over the defeated populace. They no doubt constitute either a puppet government or a colonial authority. In either case, they are in charge and they exercise that charge with severity. In such straits, the conquered and occupied people have no recourse. They are at the mercy of their wardens. Such a turn of political and social events is described elsewhere in the Israelite tradition as one of the four situations that cause the earth to tremble (cf. Prov 30:21-22).

Two verses describe the gravity of the famine that threatens the vanquished people (vv. 9-10). The "sword in the wilderness" (v. 9) is probably the weapon of those who live on the fringes of the city and who rob the poor people of the little bread that they are able to procure. The poet further compares the famine that the stricken people face with the desert's scorching heat (v. 10). It burns them with a fury like that of a solar oven and the lifeless air that it produces. Their skin is blackened and withered by the force of it.

Famine grips the people and threatens their very existence.

Up to this point, the poet has provided glimpses of some of the tribulations endured by the entire citizenry (vv. 2-10). The focus now turns to the sufferings of certain groups of people within the population. The text says that the women and maidens have been humiliated (v. 11). The verb implies that they were raped. Though it is truly a sexual offense, such ravishing is primarily a crime of power and violence. The woman is a victim of an overpowering attack. In patriarchal societies such as ancient Israel, rape was also a crime against the integrity of the entire nation. Reproductive potential of women was one of the most prized treasures of the family. In order to safeguard the continuity of the bloodline, the men of the family guarded that treasure assiduously. Rape not only violated the women, but it also shamed the men responsible for them, and it polluted the family bloodline. Rape defiled the integrity of the family itself.

The women were not the only ones who were assaulted and humiliated. Princes, those who possessed the primary responsibility of governance and through whom dynastic rule passed, are ignominiously hanged (v. 12a), and the elders or revered local leaders are treated without the honor due them (v. 12b). They have left the gates of the city where they once conducted much of its business (v. 14a). Grinding grain and carrying heavy loads were usually done by slave girls (see Exod 11:5). Young boys, the pride of the nation, are now forced to perform such demeaning work (v. 13a), trading in the stringed instruments with which they once made joyful music (v. 14b) for ponderous millstones and staggering loads of wood (v. 13b).

Each picture of torment and distress is compounded by another and yet another until the flood of negative emotion erupts. The world of the inhabitants has been turned upside down and inside out:

joy   has ceased
dancing   has been turned to mourning (v. 15)

In addition to the profound grief, there is the humiliating loss of honor. The crown, though clearly part of the attire of royalty, is also a symbol of prestige and glory. To say that the crown has fallen from one's head is to admit that one is suffering disgrace (v. 16*a*; cf. Job 19:9). Finally, introduced by an expression of utter dejection, "Woe to us," the cause of all of the heartrending misery is given: "We have sinned!" (v. 16*b*). From the point of view of retribution, this statement explains everything. It is an admission of the people's complicity in the guilt of their ancestors (v. 7), and it is an exoneration of God.

By means of a parallel construction, the poet underscores the state of affairs engendered by the tribulations enumerated in this lament (vv. 2-16):

| because | of this | our hearts | are sick |
| because | of these | our eyes | are dimmed |

Their troubles have taken all of the joy out of life; their hearts are sick with grief. Their troubles have extinguished the light from their days; their eyes are dimmed. The final blow is the worst of all. Mount Zion, a reference to the temple which was built on that high hill, now lies in ruins. After being desecrated by nonbelievers, it is destroyed (v. 18). The precincts that once teemed with devout worshipers have become the haunt of wild jackals that roam through them in search of carrion. This holy place has been profaned, and God has departed from the sanctuary. The lament ends on a note of both dishonor and despair.

You Reign Forever: 5:19

Exegetical Analysis

The communal lament moves from expressions of complaint (vv. 2-18) to an acknowledgment of the sovereignty of God (v. 19). Although there is no explicit avowal of confidence here, as is generally found in such laments, the grounds for such confidence are clearly stated. It is rooted in the conviction that God rules forever. Such a proclamation redirects our attention from the devastated temple in Zion, from which God had reigned on earth in the past, to the divine throne in heaven from which God reigns forever. The enthronement of God in heaven was one aspect of ancient creation theology. After the primeval battle between the cosmic forces of good and evil, the victorious deity established the order of creation. This order was thought to be eternal, extending back before the beginning of time and forward to beyond its end. Above this newly ordered creation the victor was then enthroned as divine-king.

When the people declare that God is enthroned forever, they are proclaiming their faith in this eternal sovereignty. The desecration and razing of the temple in Jerusalem may suggest to them the end of God's reign on earth, but they still maintain God's universal dominion in heaven. This belief is the grounds for their continued trust in God's power. The existence of divine rule is not questioned here. At issue is whether or not God's rule will favor this people.

RESTORE US: 5:20-22

Exegetical Analysis

The undisputed rule of God, ordinarily a source of confidence and praise, only engenders a final accusation:

Why   have you forgotten us   completely
         forsaken us   these many days (v. 20)

The accusation against God, which takes an interrogative form, repeats the sentiment with which the poem began: "Remember, O LORD . . . look and see" (v. 1). As stated above, there is no question about divine sovereignty itself. It is God's mercy toward the suffering people that is under scrutiny. With a twofold plea, the community cries out: Why . . . How long? Why have you forgotten us? How long will you forsake us? This prayer does not end on a note of accusation and complaint. Instead, the community turns immediately to humble petition: "Restore us to yourself." They know that it is not enough for them to return to God; such restoration is out of their hands. Only God can turn them around. This is not a prayer for the restoration of their city or its prosperity. It is a plea for a restoration to their former covenantal relationship.

The final verse of this poem (v. 22) continues to be a source of extensive scholarly discussion. First, there is disagreement over its exact translation. Then, regardless of how it is translated, its meaning is a cause of great concern because it seems to end on such a depressing note. This second point is quite significant, because these final sentiments bring to conclusion not only the communal lament of the fifth chapter but the book of Lamentations as a whole.

The verse opens with a Hebrew expression *(kî 'im)*, literally translated "for if." This construction suggests that the first half-line is a conditional clause and the second is the consequence of the condition:

> For if you have utterly rejected us,
> you are angry with us beyond measure

This reading would have the book conclude in a way that seems to be incomplete. Is this indeed the case? Has God utterly rejected the people, because of unbounded anger? The expression has also been rendered "unless." Those who prefer this translation link the verse with the preceding one (v. 21). They maintain that a condition is attached to the prayer for restoration:

> Restore us . . .
> Unless you have utterly rejected us,
> and are angry with us beyond measure

This second reading leaves the mercy of God and the restoration of the people not only undecided but even questionable. In yet another version, the expression is translated as the adversative conjunction "but":

> But you have utterly rejected us,
> and are angry with us beyond measure

This version yields a reading that is least hopeful. It suggests that restoration will not occur, because God has utterly rejected them and is angry beyond measure.

The fact that this poem concludes without some resolution of the inner struggle of the people has been the cause of great consternation. There is in this verse neither an expression of hope nor one of confidence; there is no promise of restoration or even reconciliation. In a sense, such an ending has left the question of resolution for the reader to answer: just how is one to under-stand the verse, the poem, even the entire book? Some believe that the integrity of the honest, despairing complaint with which the book is occupied would be compromised if this ending were emended. Others maintain that the lack of resolution suggests a dating of the book sometime within the exile, before the nation had been restored and its actual situation resolved. Several Hebrew versions of the book, in keeping with Jewish synagogue practice, repeat the prayer found in verse 21 at the conclusion of verse 22. (This same technique is applied to the conclusions of the books of Isaiah, Malachi, and Ecclesiastes.) In this way, the liturgical reading of the chapter, and the book in general, ends with a prayer of petition. Whichever translation and ending is preferred, most commentators still consider this chapter a com-munal lament.

Theological and Ethical Analysis

This final chapter of the book (5:1-22) invites the reader to reflect on various important themes. The first is the character of prayer to God. The assortment of prayer forms found in the Bible, particularly in the Psalms, demonstrates the variety of reli-gious sentiments that prompt one to turn to God in prayer. Although the largest group is the lament, prayers of confidence are also found in abundance (see Psalms 31, 116, 144). Such sen-timents can been found in the final poem of Lamentations. At the end of all their complaints and accusations, the people bring their brokenness to God. They do not ask for anything specific. Instead, they simply ask to be remembered, to be considered. There is an element of faith that prompts them to believe that, as was the case with their ancestors of old [cf. Exod 2:23-25; 3:7-9]), God cannot long be indifferent to their suffering. What they do not know or cannot begin to imagine is the way that God will answer their prayer.

The second theme is the issue of transmitted guilt, specifically, one generation having to suffer the consequences of the sinful-ness of another. While this may appear to be unfair according to contemporary standards of justice, it does correspond to an ancient Israelite understanding: "I the LORD your God am a jealous God, punishing children for the iniquities of parents to the third and the fourth generation of those who reject me" (Exod 20:5; Deut 5:9). Just as in modern society children inherit the wealth or poverty of parents, so in societies possessing a deep sense of communal identity, they inherit family honor or guilt as well. However, later prophets challenge this perspective: "In those days they shall no longer say: 'The parents have eaten sour grapes, and the children's teeth are set on edge'" (Jer 31:29; Ezek 18:2).

A third theme present in this passage is the ethical implications of occupation of one country by another. More than anywhere else in the book, this poem sketches some of the humiliation that accompanies the experience of being occupied by a conquering nation. It describes how those who have been vanquished are subjected to further abasement and deprivation. Rather than being given the opportunity to rebuild their lives, they are demeaned and kept in a kind of servitude. This reflects a particular military strategy wherein the conqueror keeps the vanquished subservient lest they regroup their energies and once again become a formidable threat. Such a policy raises ethical questions that can only be addressed within the historical and sociopolitical context of the nations involved. However, the poem expresses the sentiments of the conquered, sentiments that incline the reader to be sympathetic to the afflicted people.

Finally, the poem addresses the theme of the eternal reign of God. Acknowledging that the governance of the world is in the hands of God can be both disturbing and comforting. It is disturbing when women and men perceive God primarily as a strict arbiter of justice and they feel that they have been unfairly afflicted. At times like these their cry, "Why has God done this?" (Job 10:2) is more an angry challenge rising from overwhelming pain than it is a question seeking comprehension. The notion of God's eternal reign is comforting when people are convinced that God is gracious and loving and committed to human well-being (see Ps 98:1-3). It is such an assurance that enables them to endure great hardship even when they do not understand it, for they may believe that God will not abandon them in their misfortune but will draw good from the suffering. These differing points of view might be characterized as "expecting" and "accepting." In the first instance, when people have gained insight into the cause-and-effect relationship of so much of their experience, they *expect* to be able to understand how life itself works. In such situations they might view the mystery of life as merely something they have not yet uncovered. In the second instance, they might realize that they do not and probably never will be able to understand the workings of the world, and so they *accept* the limitations of human comprehension and stand in awe before life's mysteries (cf. Job 42:1-6).

It is generally only in a story being told that one can know its ending. People who have been engrossed in the story may not agree with this ending, but at least they usually recognize it. The ending of the poem in this chapter reflects life as it is being lived, not merely as it unfolded in the past. The curtain has not yet come down on the final act of the drama of life. The people whose prayer to God is contained within this final chapter are not sure of their outcome. Despite their confession of guilt, their proclamation of faith in God's power, and their presumed trust in God's care for them, they do not know with certainty how God will respond to their prayer. Will God heed their plea or disregard it? And if God does respond, will it be with tender mercy or with exacting retribution? Too often in the face of tragedy people glibly say: Everything is going to be all right; I promise you! The poet of this prayer does not offer such cheap assurance. The prayer may be heartrending, but it is also true to life. The people do not really know what their future holds. Their prayer to God ends with a plea for restoration and a realization that all is in the hands of God.

CONCLUSION

R egardless of how much is said about the poetry found in the book of Lamentations, more meaning can always be uncovered. This is true for various reasons. First, there is the rich and multifaceted nature of the imagery used to describe the wretched situation of the city and her inhabitants. The artistry of the poet(s) has crafted scenes that mesmerize readers. They continually call out to be pondered and their meaning plumbed. Each new scrutiny reveals aspects of the imagery previously undetected. Second, the enormity of the devastation depicted prevents the readers from capturing its scope in a single consideration. Too much occurred in too many dimensions of experience for them to absorb at once even a fraction of the horror. Furthermore, the destruction depicted is multilayered and it sometimes takes a while to realize the diverse and long-reaching consequences that must have flowed from it. Finally, the developing insight of women and men make them more and more sensitive to the human toll exacted by this tragic event. Therefore, each time they read Lamentations, its poetry can make a new and lasting impact on them.

The atrocities depicted in the pages of this book not only fill readers with a sense of horror and profound sadness, but they also raise several searing questions: Why would anyone inflict such tribulations on another people? What is the responsibility of those who may not be personally afflicted but who witness or become aware of these tribulations? And finally: In the face of such horror, what are people to think of God? The poems do address such questions, although they may not answer them satisfactorily.

Why are people so afflicted? Because in the fragmented world in which they live, individuals, cities, and nations are enemies to each other. Such a simple answer does not excuse the violence and destruction portrayed in the book. It merely explains it. The poems do not provide reasons for enmity, but they certainly depict some of its consequences. Entire populations are swept away in the wake of destruction brought on by rivalry and hatred. No distinction is made between those whose policies may have precipitated the enmity and the innocent and helpless. Buildings may be considered collateral damage, but people are always victims. Again and again, the poems describe such victimization.

What might be the response of those who witness such ravaging? The narrator demonstrates two major responses. The first, and perhaps most significant response, is the actual telling of the story. Victims of the Nazi holocaust have repeatedly reported that one of the major incentives for survival was the need to tell the world just what happened to them. Since ordinary women and men were implicated in the torment that they endured, it is important to realize that the seeds of such brutality and indifference may be dormant within the minds and hearts of other ordinary women and men. As the readers of Lamentations stand aghast at the torment described, the narrator raises their consciousness regarding the brutality and indifference of which human nature generally is capable.

A second response of those who witness such victimization is solidarity with the victims and empathy at the sight of their afflictions. This may have been natural for the narrator who seems to have been a compatriot of the suffering inhabitants. Still, the more women and men realize that they are all members of the same human race, that they are all inhabitants of the same earth community, that they are all children of the same caring God, they will realize that the pain of one is the pain of all. As such realization deepens within them, indifference toward the affliction of others will ebb. The narrator demonstrates solidarity with the victims.

Once the human heart has been genuinely touched by the suffering of others, often the next question asked is: What can I do? The book of Lamentations does not move into this realm. The narrator does not suggest strategies for addressing the needs of the despairing people. Still, if readers see this book as a metaphor for the plight of any city and its populace, they might be moved to examine their own hearts and the circumstances of their lives in order to discover how they might come to the aid of people who so desperately need their help.

Finally, what does such disaster say about God? Is God exercising harsh judgment, even on the innocent and the helpless? Is God disinterested, standing by while an enemy runs unrestrained over an entire city? Is God powerless to prevent the catastrophe or, once it has been inflicted, unable to offer a remedy or some form of solace? These are the questions that are left unanswered in the book. Some might say that they are questions that challenge the integrity of God, of at least a generally held perception of that integrity.

There is another way of understanding the fact that the questions are left unanswered. It is the unqualified authenticity of the book's testimony. The unresolved dilemma of suffering corresponds faithfully with the experience of human beings in the throes of suffering. In such circumstances, even dedicated believers wonder where God is. Their faith may not provide them with an adequate explanation, and their trust in God does not guarantee consolation. When the world within which they live collapses around them, the world of meaning within them is also undermined. This is the point to which the book brings its readers. It enables them to grieve with the people of the city, to accuse enemies and to accuse God. But there it stops. It is up to the reader to take the next step. Will it be a step into total despair, or one into trust in the mystery that is God? Will it be a step into further self-absorption, or one into commitment to social responsibility? The book of Lamentations is not only a challenge to read and understand, it is a book that provides its readers with a challenge for living.

SELECT BIBLIOGRAPHY

COMMENTARIES

Dobbs-Allsopp, F. W., 2002. *Lamentations. Interpretation: A Bible Commentary for Teaching and Preaching.* Louisville: Westminster/John Knox. A somewhat technical commentary that allows the voice of suffering to be heard loud and clear.

Hillers, Delbert R. 1992. *Lamentations.* Anchor Bible 7A, second revised edition. New York: Doubleday. An excellent critical commentary intended for a general audience. It provides primarily literary analysis of the text but also information of possible historical background.

O'Connor, Kathleen M. 2001. "The Book of Lamentations: Introduction, Commentary, and Reflections." *The New Interpreter's Bible* Vol. VI, Leander E. Keck, et al., eds. 1013-1072. Nashville: Abingdon Press. Provides not only critical commentary, but also profound theological reflection on the message. Written with the general audience in view.

_____. 2002. *Lamentations and the Tears of the World.* Maryknoll: Orbis. A commentary that treats the the descriptions of destruction and dashed hopes with honesty and sensitivity. Her theological reflections engage elements from the book with issues in the contemporary world.

Provan, Iain. 1991. *Lamentations.* The New Century Bible Commentary. Grand Rapids: Eerdmans. A brief but insightful commentary that emphasizes literary analysis and suggests an innovative historical perspective.

Reyburn, William D. 1992. *A Handbook on Lamentations*. UBS Handbook Series. New York: United Bible Society. Intended for translations, it offers both a careful explanation of the text and suggestions for conveying the ideas in various ways.

Westermann, Claus. 1994. *Lamentations: Issues and Interpretation* (trans. Charles Meunchow). Minneapolis: Fortress Press. A careful literary analysis of the book with an extensive introductory summary of studies that offer different explanations of the genre of the book.

SELECTED STUDIES

Albrektson, Bertil. 1963. *Studies in the Text and Theology of the Book of Lamentations*. Studia Theologica Lundensia 21. Lund: CWK Gleerup. A very technical study of the Hebrew text and comparisons of that text with those of the Septuagint and the Peshitta.

Berlin, Adele. 2002. *Lamentations*. The Old Testament Library. Louisville: Westminster/John Knox. A critical literary poetic approach that draws heavily on feminist critique.

Dobbs-Allsopp, F. W. 1993. *Weep, O Daughter of Zion: A Study of the City-Lament Genre in the Hebrew Bible*. Biblica et Orientalia 44. Roma: Editrice Pontificio Istituto Biblico. A careful study of the city-lament genre which highlights both similarities and differences between the Mesopotamian form and the biblical tradition.

_____. 1997. "Tragedy, Tradition, and Theology in the Book of Lamentations." *Journal for the Study of the Old Testament* 74, 29-60. A "tragic" reading of the Lamentations, which reading is then used to show the book's distinctiveness.

Freedman, David Noel, 1986. "Acrostic Poems in the Hebrew Bible: Alphabetic and Otherwise." *Catholic Biblical Quarterly* 48, 408-31. A detailed study of the topic with some attention given to the book of Lamentations.

Garr, W. Randall. 1983. "The *Qinah*: A Study of Poetic Meter, Syntax and Style." *Zeitschrift für die alttestamentliche Wissenschaft* 95, 54-75. A technical explanation of characteristics of the *qinah* structure, its meaning and functions in various poetic sections of the Old Testament.

Gerstenberger, Erhard S. 2001. *Psalms, Part 2, and Lamentations.* Grand Rapids: Eerdmans. A discussion of the structure, genre, setting, and meaning of the books in question.

Gottwald, Norman K. 1954. *Studies in the Book of Lamentations* (SBT). Chicago: Alec R. Allenson. A study of the literary character and theological significance of the book of Lamentations.

_____. 1993. "The Book of Lamentations Reconsidered." In *The Hebrew Bible in its Social World and in Ours.* Atlanta: Scholars Press, 165-73. An addendum to his 1962 work *Studies in the Book of Lamentations* in which he updates literary, tradition-historical, and sociological perspectives.

Grossberg, Daniel. 1989. *Centripetal and Centrifugal Structures in Biblical Poetry.* Society of Biblical Literature Monograph Series 39. Atlanta: Scholars Press. A technical treatment of poetic techniques found in Lamentations and compared with these techniques found in other biblical literature.

Hunter, Jannie. 1996. *Faces of a Lamenting City: The Development and Coherence of the book of Lamentations.* Frankfort: Peter Lang. A thorough discussion of the contents and development of the Book of Lamentations which uses intertextuality as the major strategy of interpretation.

Johnson, Bo. 1985. "Form and Message in Lamentations." *Zeitschrift für die alttestamentliche Wissenschaft* 85, 58-73. An argument in favor of a chiastic interpretation of the book, which would place the heart of the book's meaning in chapter 3.

Kaiser, Barbara Bakke. 1987. "Poet as 'Female Impersonator': The Image of Daughter Zion as Speaker in Biblical Poems of Suffering." *Journal of Religion* 87, 164-82. The poet follows the lead of Jeremiah in using a female voice to describe the misery experienced by the city Zion and its inhabitants.

Kramer, S. N. 1959. "Sumerian Literature and the Bible." *Studia biblica et Orientalia: 3 Oriens Antiquus* (Analecta Biblica 12), 201. A comparison of the picture of Assyrian goddesses weeping over the ruin of their sanctuaries and personified Zion in the face of the destruction of her city.

Lanahan, William F. 1974. "The Speaking Voice in the Book of Lamentations." *Journal of Biblical Literature* 93, 41-9. The author argues for five distinct voices in the book of Lamentations, each one dominating one of the five chapters of the book.

Linafelt, Tod. 1997. *Surviving Lamentations: Catastrophe, Lament, and Protest in the Afterlife of a Biblical Book.* Chicago: University of Chicago. A careful and thorough study of issues that surround survival. It reviews literature, particularly Holocaust and postmodern authors, who describe experiences of actual survival as well as ways that readers "survive" literal or metaphorical descriptions of horror.

Mintz, Alan. 1982. "The Rhetoric of Lamentations and the Representation of Catastrophe." *Prooftexts* 2, 3-17. An explanation of how the form of lament addresses social and religious catastrophe and the human suffering that it engenders.

Owens, Pamela Jean. 1990. "Personification and Suffering in Lamentations 3." *Austin Seminary Bulletin* (Faculty Edition), 75-90. A discussion of the personifications of the city as woman in great torment and of God as a brutal enemy.

Renkema, Johan. 1988. "The Literary Structure of Lamentations." *The Structural Analysis of Biblical and Canaanite Poetry*, ed. W. Van der Meer & J. C. de Moor. *Journal for the Study of the Old Testament* Supplement Series 74. Sheffield: Sheffield Academic Press, 294-396. A technical study of both the external (acrostic) and internal (chiastic) structures of the book.

Shea, William. 1979. "The *qinah* Structure of the Book of Lamentations." *Biblica* 60, 103-7. A straightforward explanation of the *qinah* meter, its appearance in the poetic lines of the book of Lamentations, and the role that this structure may play in the overall structure of the book.